to Bob & Pam

Christmas 2001.

GW00342000

# THE PLEASURES
# OF THE TABLE

I look upon it, that he who
does not mind his belly will
hardly mind anything else.
*Samuel Johnson*

*By the same editor*

The Gardener's Quotation Book
The Marriage Quotation Book
The Gourmet Quotation Book
The Wine Quotation Book
The Traveller's Quotation Book
The Pleasures of Love

# The Pleasures of the Table

Edited by
JENNIFER TAYLOR

ROBERT HALE · LONDON

ISBN 0 7090 5232 4

Robert Hale Limited
Clerkenwell House
Clerkenwell Green
London EC1R 0HT

## For my mother

Photoset in North Wales by
Derek Doyle & Associates, Mold, Clwyd.
Printed and bound in Great Britain by
WBC Ltd, Bridgend, Mid-Glamorgan.

# Contents

# *Preface*

eading old cookery books or accounts of scrumptious food eaten, in memoirs and diaries, often makes one wonder what exactly the food tasted like. Because of different cooking methods it undoubtedly tasted different, with for instance shorter cooking times for roasting poultry and game over a spit than would be needed for oven roasting now. And because palates were attuned to the salt and spices used for preserving, or for masking odours, the flavour was probably more intense.

Gourmets of old certainly went in for extravagantly elaborate dishes. It would be a culinary experience to make up Brillat-Savarin's recipe for pheasant – stuffed with minced woodcock, bacon and truffles, placed on slices of bread spread with the woodcock's liver pounded with truffles, and served with bitter oranges. No wonder palates became jaded and yearned for plainer food.

In his book *La Physiologie du goût*, Brillat-Savarin also drools over the aroma of roasting quails; shot in the wild, these birds were certainly plumper and probably gamier than the skinny little things sold in supermarkets. Was the quality of the ingredients in general higher? Some things undoubtedly *were* better

in the past, and country people who had access to fresh foodstuffs grown locally, or their own garden produce, must have fed very wholesomely indeed. The supply of foodstuffs to towns, with so much scope for adulteration along the way, was a different matter. In *Humphrey Clinker*, Tobias Smollett evoked the 'bread sweet and nourishing', the 'mutton fed on the fragrant herbage of the mountains', the 'trout and salmon struggling from the stream' that came to his table in the country, and contrasted it all with the vile bread and milk, stinking fish and nauseous beer that were on offer in London.

It seems that it has always been too much to expect that food should be simply food, *real* food. Today, quite apart from the array of manufactured ersatz items and all the unnecessary tampering done, there are so many food scares that it sometimes seems as though nothing is completely safe: beef, French cheese, eggs, shellfish from polluted waters and fruit contaminated with chemicals, everything has come under suspicion.

And yet there is of course so much to be thankful for. Better the blandness of some modern foodstuffs than rotten meat and eggs. And the huge range of food now available is amazing.

It is certainly a human characteristic to imagine that things were better in the past. When I think back to my childhood, the strongest culinary memory I

have is the smell of onions frying gently in creamy Swiss butter (oodles of it) with succulent veal chops to follow. My French grandmother, for she was the cook just throwing things into the pan, lived in Switzerland, so that childhood holidays were a culinary paradise for impressionable young tastebuds after the shortages of glum fifties' England. There were tender *filets mignons* of beef, really thick cream which could be beaten to glistening peaks or into exquisitely light *fontainebleaus*, honey redolent of fir trees and wildflowers, while the apricots and peaches picked a few hours down the line in the Valais seemed to burst with sunshine. (We walked off all this with daylong rambles up and down mountain paths; but Switzerland is of course notable for its mountaintop restaurants, so a meringue with whipped cream was often the reward for a morning's arduous climb.)

The importance of diet was recognized centuries ago, but still the medical establishment cannot make its mind up about various matters. As more scientific facts become established, it seems that a lot of plain commonsense gets forgotten.

It was the good Mrs Beeton who opined that a healthy person, with good exercise, should have a fresh supply of food once every four hours. Many would say this is overstating the case, but it is not so far out.

At all events, eating, or not eating (i.e. dieting) takes up a lot of human endeavour. It seems an innocent pleasure to enjoy good food, but it is by no means a universal predilection. Eating is for some a purely mechanical function which leaves them indifferent, while from others it attracts censoriousness. Bernard Levin, who has many a time shared the details of sumptuous meals with his *Times* readers,

 once revealed that he never received so much hate mail as after he had written one of these pieces.

Let us for now share in the enjoyment of those who have recorded so evocatively the pleasures of the table – from an elegant dinner at the Rothschilds to simple food eaten with a hearty appetite. There are many passages from Dickens showing the diversity of eating experiences; there is Virginia Woolf enjoying lunch in a college hall; Arnold Bennett overdoing the wine and liqueurs at a Paris restaurant; Byron complaining about his digestion; Haydn missing the delicacies of Vienna; and Casanova exploiting the full potential of eating oysters.

And since so much in human affairs remains constant, the complaints – about stale and badly cooked food, and sloppy service in restaurants – are still relevant today.

JENNIFER TAYLOR

10

# The Joys of Food

The pleasures of the table are common to all times and all ages, to every country and every day; they harmonize with all our other pleasures, and outlive them to console us for their loss.

BRILLAT-SAVARIN
*La Physiologie du goût*

We may talk sentiment as much as we like, but the stomach is the real seat of happiness in this world. The kitchen is the chief temple wherein we worship, its roaring fire is our vestal flame, and the cook is our great high-priest. He is a mighty magician and a kindly one. He soothes away all sorrow and care. He drives forth all enmity, gladdens all love. Our God is great, and the cook is his prophet.

JEROME K. JEROME
*The Idle Thoughts of an Idle Fellow*

Love of food and love of God are probably synonymous. If you love life, you love food.

DELIA SMITH

11

I am no Quaker at my food. I confess I am not indifferent to the kinds of it. Those unctuous morsels of deer's flesh were not made to be received with dispassionate services.

CHARLES LAMB
*The Essays of Elia*


You needn't tell me that a man who doesn't love oysters and asparagus and good wines has got a soul or a stomach either. He's simply got the instinct for being unhappy highly developed.

SAKI
*The Chronicles of Clovis*


Sensuous pleasures, like eating and drinking, are sometimes described as animal, and therefore unworthy. It must be confessed, however, that men, are, in this life, animals all through ... and that they have a right to enjoy without reproach those pleasures of animal existence which maintain health, strength, and life itself.

CHARLES W. ELIOT
*The Happy Life*, 1896


A man who brags regarding himself that whatever he swallows is the same to him, and that his coarse palate recognizes no difference between venison and turtle, pudding, or mutton-broth, as his indifferent jaws close over them, brags about a personal defect, and not about a virtue. It is like a man boasting that he has no ear for music, or no eye for colour, or that his nose cannot scent the difference between a rose and a cabbage.

W.M. THACKERAY
*Miscellaneous Papers*

13

The only way in which good humour can be secured for humanity is by habitual good eating.

> FORD MADOX FORD
> *Provence*

An empty stomach produces an empty brain; our mind, independent as it may appear to be, respects the laws of digestion, and we may say … that good thoughts proceed from the stomach.

> HONORÉ DE BALZAC

The human frame being what it is, heart, body and brain all mixed together …, a good dinner is of great importance to good talk. One cannot think well, love well, sleep well, if one has not dined well. The lamp in the spine does not light on beef and prunes.

> VIRGINIA WOOLF
> *A Room of One's Own*

Thought depends absolutely on the stomach, but in spite of that, those who have the best stomachs are not the best thinkers.

> VOLTAIRE

A man may be a pessimistic determinist before lunch and an optimistic believer in the will's freedom after it.

> ALDOUS HUXLEY
> *Do What You Will*

People who have tried it, tell me that a clear conscience makes you very happy and contented; but a full stomach does the business quite as well, and is cheaper, and more easily obtained. One feels so forgiving and generous after a substantial and well-digested meal …

It is very strange this domination of our intellect by our digestive organs. We cannot work, we cannot think, unless our stomach wills so. It dictates to us our emotions, our passions. After eggs and bacon, it says, 'Work!' After beefsteak and porter it says, 'Sleep!' …

Reach not after morality and righteousness, my friends; watch vigilantly your stomach, and diet it with care and judgement. Then virtue and contentment will come and reign within your heart …; and you will be a good citizen, a loving husband, and a tender father – a noble, pious man.

> JEROME K. JEROME
> *Three Men in a Boat*

How many ill-natured words, quarrels, suits in the Divorce Courts, and even murders, have originated over a badly-cooked dinner? How many happy marriages, how many hard-and-fast friendships have been formed over a nicely cooked dinner?

> words from *Punch*, 1875

The humour I am in is worse than words can describe. I have had a hideous dinner of some abominable spiced-up indescribable mess, and it has exasperated me against the world at large.

> CHARLOTTE BRONTË
> in a letter to Ellen Nussey, 17 October 1841

Recognizing, then, that there are higher pleasures than eating and drinking, let us clearly perceive that three meals a day all one's life not only give in themselves a constantly renewed innocent satisfaction, but provide the necessary foundation for all other satisfactions.

> CHARLES W. ELIOT
> *The Happy Life*, 1896

We do not eat alone, but in families, or sets of friends and comrades; and the table is the best centre of friendships and of the domestic affections.

CHARLES W. ELIOT
*The Happy Life*, 1896

Once a week is quite enough to dine with one's own relations.

OSCAR WILDE
*The Importance of Being Earnest*

To enjoy food and rejoice in feminine beauty is only to be human.

CONFUCIUS

We were the sort of family who would be talking about dinner while we were eating lunch.

MICHEL ROUX

# Gourmets, Gourmands and Gluttons

It is certainly odd that Englishmen should have an exalted idea of the sense of taste that they bestow its name upon the faculty of estimating all that is most sublime and beautiful in nature and art, while they have no name left for the fine appreciation of food, for the enjoyments of the table, ... which does not confuse dining with gorging and the gratification of the palate with the repletion of a sot.

E.S. DALLAS
*Kettner's Book of the Table*, 1877

To make a god of one's stomach is despicable, but the eunuchs of taste are as much to pity as those of the seraglio: the first lack a palate, and we know what is lacking in the others. Galanterie is not debauchery, and the gourmet is not a glutton.

LUCIEN TENDRET
*La Table au pays de Brillat-Savarin*, 1892

I could mention the most august names of poets, statesmen, philosophers, historians, judges, and divines, who are as great at the dinner-table as in the field, the closet, the senate, or the bench … I have sat at table with a great, world-renowned statesman. I watched him during the progress of the banquet – I am at liberty to say that he enjoyed it like a man.

On another day, it was a celebrated literary character. It was beautiful to see him at his dinner: cordial and generous, jovial and kindly, the great author enjoyed himself as the great statesman – may he long give us good books and good dinners!

Yet another day, and I sat opposite to a Right Reverend Bishop. My Lord, I was pleased to see good thing after good thing disappear before you; and think no man ever better became that rounded episcopal apron. How amiable he was; how kind! He put water into his wine. Let us respect the moderation of the Church.

And then the men learned in the law: how they dine! what hospitality, what splendour, what comfort, what wine!

W.M. THACKERAY
*Travels in London*, 1853

The sin of gourmandise, although classified among the seven deadly sins, is the one for which the Church most readily grants absolution, knowing only too well its irresistible seduction.

GRIMOD DE LA REYNIÈRE
*Calendrier gastronomique*

18

The appearance of dinner, which consisted of a variety of dishes, seemed to diffuse new cheerfulness upon every face; so that I now expected the philosophical conversation to begin, as they improved in good humour. The principal priest, however, opened his mouth with only observing that the venison had not been kept enough, though he had given strict orders for having it killed ten days before. 'I fear,' continued he, 'it will be found to want the true healthy flavour: you will find nothing of the original wildness in it.' A priest, who sat next to him, having smelt it and wiped his nose: 'Ah, my good lord,' cries he, 'you are too modest, it is perfectly fine; everybody knows that nobody understands keeping venison with your lordship.'

OLIVER GOLDSMITH
a visitation dinner, *The Citizen of the World*


I remember dining once with no less than nine doctors; they all ate turtle soup, they all took curry, they all drank champagne and port afterwards, they all had liqueurs with their *demie-tasse*, and they all smoked. I was not present, either at the post-mortem or at the inquest.

GEORGE AUGUSTUS SALA
*The Thorough Good Cook*, 1895


Financiers are the heroes of gourmandise.

BRILLAT-SAVARIN
*La Physiologie du goût*


Foodies are typically an aspiring professional couple to whom food is a fashion.

ANN BARR and PAUL LEVY
*The Official Foodie Handbook*

Gluttony is ranked with the deadly sins; it should be honoured among the cardinal virtues ... Gross are they who see in eating and drinking nought but grossness. Gluttony is a vice only when it leads to stupid, inartistic excess.

ELIZABETH PENNELL
*The Feasts of Autolycus*, The Story of a Greedy Woman, 1896


Great food is like great sex – the more you have the more you want.

GAIL GREENE
American food critic


O glotonye, ful of cursednesse!
O cause first of oure confusioun!
O original of oure dampnacioun,
Til Crist hadde boght us with his blood agayn!

GEOFFREY CHAUCER
'The Pardoner's Tale', *The Canterbury Tales*


*Gourmand*: A glutton; a greedy eater.

SAMUEL JOHNSON
*Dictionary*


Many a day did he fast, many a year did he refrain from wine; but when he did eat, it was voraciously; when he did drink wine, it was copiously. He could practise abstinence, but not temperance.

JAMES BOSWELL
*Life of Johnson*


A greedy man God hates.

OLD SCOTS PROVERB

With his well padded stomach, the true gourmand can consume a large quantity of wine. He has a four bottle advantage at least on the drinker without appetite.

GRIMOD DE LA REYNIÈRE
*Almanach des gourmands*

Eat-well is drink-well's brother.
THOMAS FULLER
*Gnomologia*

The way one eats is the way one works.
CZECH PROVERB

She was always eating, and always eating too much. If I went there in the morning, there was the horrid familiar odour of those oniony sandwiches; if in the afternoon, dinner had been just removed, and I was choked by reeking reminiscences of roast-meat. Tea we have spoken of … She gobbled up more cakes than any six people present; then came the supper and the sandwiches again …

She was as thin as ever, paler if possible than ever: but, by heavens! her nose began to grow red!

W.M. THACKERAY
*The Fitz-Boodle Papers*

He saw a Man who was a Soldier eat a hind-Quarter of Veal that weighed eighteen Pounds, a sixpenny Loaf of Bread, and drank three Quarts of Beer, at one Meal for a Wager.

REVD JAMES WOODFORDE
*Diary*, 14 October 1795

Without doubt, the most of mankind grossly overeat themselves; our meals serve not only for support, but as a hearty and natural diversion from the labour of life.

ROBERT LOUIS STEVENSON
*Travels with a Donkey in the Cévennes*

Louis XVIII was not only a great epicure as to the *recherche* of his dinners, but had also a surprising appetite; he has been known at table, in the interval between the first and second courses, of which he always partook largely, to have a *plat* of little pork cutlets, dressed in a particular manner, handed to him by one of the pages; and he would take them up one by one in his fingers, and before the second service was arranged the contents of his little *plat* had disappeared.

The poor duke [d'Escars] emulated his royal master in this respect … In consequence of his office he presided always at a large table served for him in the palace, the menu of which was precisely the same as that served to the king. I remember once to have seen him with his old duchess, and sundry other emigrants returned with the Restoration, who still retained their powdered heads, and who would eat almost to suffocation. When the coffee was announced, one of the old pursy gourmands would sputter out to the lady, '*Madame la Duchesse, veut elle bien me permettre de prendre un instant de sieste*'; and then he would recline in his armchair, and throw his napkin over his head and slumber for a few minutes, till nature was a little relieved.

THOMAS RAIKES
*Journal*, 26 January 1833

Stomach: the greatest of deities.
EURIPIDES

As accurately as I can calculate, between the ages of
ten and seventy, I have eaten forty-four waggon-
loads of food more than was good for me.

    REVD SYDNEY SMITH


Every ounce that a man eats more than he needs
positively weakens him, for his vegetable forces use
up his energy in getting rid of the needless food.

    FRANCIS WILLIAM NEWMAN
    *Essays on Diet*, 1883


Clogged with yesterday's excess, the body drags the
mind down with it, and fastens to the ground this
fragment of divine spirit.

    HORACE
    *Satires*


The inhabitants of cold moist countries are generally
more fat than those of warm and dry; but the most
common cause is too great a quantity of food, and too
small a quantity of motion; in plain English, gluttony
and laziness.

    JOHN ARBUTHNOT
    *An Essay Concerning the Nature of Ailments*, 1731


I have heard it remarked by a statesman of high
reputation, that most great men have died of over
eating themselves.

    HENRY TAYLOR
    *Sermons*

# Divine Digestion

The stomach is the conductor who rules the grand orchestra of our passions. An empty stomach is to me like a bassoon which growls with discontent or a piccolo flute which expresses its desire in shrill tones. A full stomach, on the other hand, is the triangle of pleasure, or the drum of joy. To eat, to love, to sing, to digest – these are, in truth, the four acts of the comic opera we call life. Who ever let it pass without having enjoyed them is a consummate ass.

ROSSINI

Sitting quiet after eating is akin to sitting still during divine service so as not to disturb the congregation.

SAMUEL BUTLER
*Note-Books, 1912*

Before he composed himself for a nap, Mr Pecksniff delivered a kind of grace after meat, in these words:

'The process of digestion, as I have been informed by anatomical friends, is one of the most wonderful works of nature. I do not know how it may be with others, but it is a great satisfaction to me to know, when regaling on my humble fare, that I am putting in motion the most beautiful machinery with which we have any acquaintance. I really feel at such times as if I was doing a public service.'

CHARLES DICKENS
*Martin Chuzzlewit*

Digestion is the great secret of life.

REVD SYDNEY SMITH
in a letter in 1837

*Digestion, n.* The conversion of victuals into virtues. When the process is imperfect, vices are evolved instead.

> AMBROSE BIERCE
> *The Enlarged Devil's Dictionary*

Digestion is the business of the stomach, indigestion that of the doctors.

> GRIMOD DE LA REYNIÈRE
> *Almanach des gourmands*

Indigestion is charged by God with enforcing morality on the stomach.

> VICTOR HUGO

His own stomach could bear nothing rich, and he could never believe other people to be different from himself. What was unwholesome to him he regarded as unfit for anybody; and he had, therefore earnestly tried to dissuade them from having any wedding-cake at all ... There was no rest for his benevolent nerves till it was all gone.

> JANE AUSTEN
> *Emma.*

How can we hope to understand anybody, knowing nothing of their stomachs?

> KATHERINE MANSFIELD
> *In a German Pension*

When we sat down to dinner I asked Byron if he would take soup? 'No, he never took soup.' – 'Would he take fish?' 'No, he never took fish.' – Presently I asked if he would eat some mutton? 'No, he never ate mutton.' – I then asked if he would take a glass of wine? 'No, he never tasted wine.' – It was now necessary to inquire what he *did* eat and drink; and the answer was, 'Nothing but hard biscuits and soda-water.' Unfortunately, neither hard biscuits nor soda-water were at hand; and he dined upon potatoes bruised down on his plate and drenched with vinegar.... Some days after, meeting Hobhouse, I said to him, 'How long will Lord Byron persevere in his present diet?' He replied, 'Just as long as you continue to notice it.' I did not then know, what I now know to be a fact – that Byron, after leaving my house, had gone to a Club in St James's Street, and eaten a hearty meat-supper.

SAMUEL ROGERS
*Table Talk*


I have dined regularly today, for the first time since Sunday last – this being Sabbath, too. All the rest, tea and dry biscuits – six *per diem*. I wish to God I had not dined now! – It kills me with heaviness, stupor, and horrible dreams; ... I wish I were in the country, to take exercise – instead of being obliged to *cool* by abstinence, in lieu of it. I should not so much mind a little accession of flesh – my bones can well bear it. But the worst is, the devil always came with it – till I starved him out, and I will *not* be the slave of *any* appetite ... Oh, my head – how it aches! – the horrors of digestion! I wonder how Buonaparte's dinner agrees with him?

LORD BYRON
in a letter, 17 November 1813


What possibly prevented Bonaparte from becoming a gourmand was the fear which pursued him constantly that towards the age of thirty or forty he would become obese ...

Far from having enriched the gastronomic repertory, the only new dish which came out of all his victories was the *Poulet à la Marengo*. Bonaparte drank but little wine, and always Bordeaux or Burgundy, his preference being for the latter. After lunch, as well as after dinner, he would take a cup of coffee. He was irregular in his meals, ate quickly and badly; but as soon as hunger made itself felt, it had to be satisfied; and his service was organized so that at any time and place he could have poultry, chops and coffee.

ALEXANDRE DUMAS
*Le Grand dictionnaire de cuisine*, 1873


The fate of a nation has often depended upon the good or bad digestion of a prime minister.

VOLTAIRE


After I came home last night my stomach was extremely disordered – with bile I suppose from unwonted late hours and change of living – so much for turtle and venison every day.

SIR WALTER SCOTT
*Journal*, 9 October 1827


Those persons who suffer from indigestion, or who become drunk, are utterly ignorant of the true principles of eating and drinking.

BRILLAT-SAVARIN
*La Physiologie du goût*


I dined with C.L. at Maire's, corner of Boulevard de Strasbourg, and really enjoyed myself. The place is very chic, and I hit on a Burgundy at 3.50 which was really fine. Naturally I drank too much of it. I finished the dinner with 'fruits rafraîchis', refreshed, that is, with abundant liqueurs such as Kirsch; I also had a little cognac. The consequence was that I was extremely unwell in the night.

ARNOLD BENNETT
*Journals*, 2 December 1903

King Henry VIII, as he was hunting in Windsor Forest, struck down about dinner-time to the Abbey of Reading, where, disguising himself, he was invited to the abbot's table, and passed for one of the King's guard. A sirloin of beef was set before him ..., on which the King laid on lustily. 'I would give an hundred pounds on the condition I could feed so heartily on beef as you do,' said the abbot. 'Alas! my weak and queasy stomach will hardly digest the leg of a small rabbit or chicken.' The King heartily thanked him for his good cheer, and after dinner departed undiscovered. Some weeks after, the abbot was sent for, brought up to London, clapt in the Tower, kept close prisoner and fed on bread and water; his mind was filled with fears, wondering how he had incurred the King's displeasure. At last a sirloin of beef was set before him, and the abbot verified the proverb that two hungry meals make the third a glutton. In springs King Henry out of a private lobby, where he had placed himself. 'My lord,' said the King, 'presently deposit your £100 in gold. I have been your physician to cure you of your queasy stomach, and I demand my fee for the same.' The abbot, glad he had escaped so, returned to Reading, somewhat lighter in his purse, but so much merrier in heart than when he had come.

anecdote recounted by THOMAS FULLER in *The Church History of Britain*, 1655

Seek an appetite by hard toil.
HORACE
*Satires*

# The Joys of Dieting

One of the greatest evils of old age is the advance of the stomach over the rest of the body. It looks like the accumulation of thousands of dinners and luncheons.

> REVD SYDNEY SMITH
> in a letter in 1840

To lengthen thy life, lessen thy meals.

> BENJAMIN FRANKLIN
> *Poor Richard*, 1733

If you wish to grow thinner, diminish your dinner,
And take to light claret instead of pale ale;
Look down with an utter contempt upon butter,
And never touch bread till it's toasted – or stale.

> HENRY LEIGH
> 'A Day for Wishing', 1869

I am making good progress – in fact, I am in a regular train of promotion. From gruel, vermicelli and sago, I was promoted to panada, from thence to minced meat, and (such is the effect of good conduct) I was elevated to a mutton-chop. If you hear any tidings of 16 or 18 lbs of human flesh, they belong to me – I look as if a curate had been taken out of me.

> REVD SYDNEY SMITH
> in a letter in 1844

I've been on a constant diet for the last two decades. I've lost a total of 789 pounds. By all accounts, I should be hanging from a charm bracelet.

> ERMA BOMBECK

I always choose the plainest food
To mend viscidity of blood.
Hail! water-gruel, healing power,
Of easy access to the poor, …
To thee I fly, by thee dilute –
Through veins my blood doth quicker shoot.
   MATTHEW GREEN
   'The Spleen', 1737


Although abstinence from meat and drink
moderately used, according to the age, constitution of
body, and time of the yeere, be very greatly available
for the preservation of health, because it abateth the
bloud, concocteth raw humors, and expelleth all
manner of superfluidities; yet if it be immoderately,
untimely and unadvisedly used, it is no lesse hurtfull
than Intemperance for it spoyleth the stomack,
destroyeth the spirits, and subverteth the strength,
and the naturall heat, by withdrawing of nutrimentall
moysture.
   TOBIAS VENNER
   *Via Recta ad Vitam Longam*, 1620


Well might poor Robert remember the devastation of
his home when Daisy, after the perusal of a little
pamphlet which she picked up on a book-stall called
*The Uric Acid Monthly*, came to the shattering
conclusion that her buxom frame consisted almost
entirely of waste-products which must be eliminated.
   E.F. BENSON
   *Queen Lucia*


I went on a diet, swore off drinking and heavy eating,
and in fourteen days I lost two weeks.
   JOE E. LEWIS

As for the [Harrogate] water which is said to have effected so many surprising cures, I have drank it once, and the first draught has cured me of all desire to repeat the medicine. Some people say it smells of rotten eggs, and others compare it to the scourings of a foul gun. It is generally supposed to be strongly impregnated with sulphur ... I was obliged to hold my nose with one hand, while I advanced the glass to my mouth with the other; and after I had made shift to swallow it my stomach could hardly retain what it had received.

>TOBIAS SMOLLETT
>*The Expedition of Humphry Clinker*

A big man is always accused of gluttony, whereas a wizened or osseous man can eat like a refugee at every meal, and no one ever notices his greed.

>ROBERTSON DAVIES
>*The Table Talk of Samuel Marchbanks*

I have never been able to sacrifice my appetite on the altar of appearance.

>ROBERT MORLEY

A gourmet who thinks of calories is like a tart who looks at her watch.

>JAMES BEARD

... octogenarians of unblemished appetite and unfailing good humor – spry, wry, and free of the ulcers that come from worrying about a balanced diet ...

>A.J. LIEBLING
>*Between Meals*

# Good Advice

Eat slowly: only men in rags
And gluttons old in sin
Mistake themselves for carpet bags
And tumble victuals in.
   SIR WALTER RALEIGH
   *Laughter from a Cloud*, 1923

Unquiet meals make ill digestions.
   WILLIAM SHAKESPEARE
   *The Comedy of Errors*

*A party of hygienic enthusiasts follow the system whereby all food is masticated eighty-five times. A Punch cartoon from 1906.*

Nature will castigate those who don't masticate.
ROBERT FLETCHER


Stop short of your appetite; eat less than you are able.
OVID
*Ars Amatoria*


Stop eating when you are enjoying it most.
GERMAN PROVERB


In eating a third of the stomach should be filled with food, a third with drink and the rest left empty.
THE TALMUD


Eat not, unlesse the appetite be certaine, and the superiour intestines empty of the meats formerly received; for it is most hurtfull to the body, to ingest nourishment upon nourishment not digested.
TOBIAS VENNER
*Via Recta ad Vitam Longam*, 1620


Their best and most wholesome feeding is upon one dish and no more and the same plain and simple: for surely this huddling of many meats one upon another of divers tastes is pestiferous. But sundry sauces are more dangerous than that.
PLINY
*Historia Naturalis*


We never repent of having eaten too little.
THOMAS JEFFERSON
*Writings*

If, after exercise, we feed sparingly, the digestion will be easy and good, the body lightsome, the temper cheerful, and all the animal functions performed agreeably.

BENJAMIN FRANKLIN
*The Art of Procuring Pleasant Dreams*


Rev. Mr Barclay I called on, and had a long conversation with him. He considers my inconvenience of feeling as arising from suppressed gouty humours. He advised a disuse of wine – particularly Port Wine – and to substitute a little Brandy & Water. To eat roasted Apples for supper, – White Biscuits instead of Bread – to avoid eating web-footed Animals – Salmon, Mackrell. To eat in preference Venison, all game, Fowls; Beef & Mutton are less to be preferred than the former. *Large* Cod, – whitings, Soles, Haddocks – Turbot, all good. To avoid Pork entirely … To regulate the Bile ought to be the great object of life – the oppressions caused by it when in a vitiated state destroys mankind. Avoid Milk, I remarked on it being the natural food of Children, and what, said He, is so bilious as a young Child … Avoid vegetables.

JOSEPH FARINGTON
*Diary*, 5 April 1797


Porridge fills the Englishman up, prunes clear him out.

E.M. FORSTER


'You see, Sir Harry,' he would say, *'it's all done by eating*! More people dig their graves with their teeth than we imagine. Not that I would deny you the good things of this world, but I would recommend a few at a time, and no mixing. No side-dishes. No liqueurs – only two or three wines. Whatever your stomach fancies *give it*! Begin now, tomorrow, with the waters. A pint before breakfast – half an hour after, tea, fried ham and eggs, brown bread, and a walk. Luncheon – another pint – a roast pigeon and fried potatoes, then a ride. Dinner at six, *not later* mind; gravy soup, glass of sherry, nice fresh turbot and lobster sauce – wouldn't recommend salmon – another glass of sherry – then a good cut out of the middle of a well-browned saddle of mutton, wash it over with a few glasses of iced champagne; and if you like a little light pastry to wind up with, well and good. A pint of old port and a devilled biscuit can hurt no man. *Mind*, no salads, or cucumbers, or celery, at dinner, or fruit after ...

With these and suchlike comfortable assurances, he pocketed his guineas, and bowed his patients out by the dozen.

R.S. SURTEES
advice from Dr Roger Swizzle, *Handley Cross*


Few persons bestow half so much attention on the preservation of their own Health, as they daily devote to that of their Dogs and Horses.

DR WILLIAM KITCHINER
*The Cook's Oracle*


'So you've given up wine and tobacco, Brown?'

'Yes, horses and dogs do very well without stimulants; so why shouldn't we?'

caption to *Punch* cartoon, 1878


Food is an important part of a balanced diet.

FRAN LEBOWITZ
*Metropolitan Life*

# On Vegetarianism

Oh, how criminal it is for flesh to be stored away in flesh, for one greedy body to grow fat with food gained from another, for one live creature to go on living through the destruction of another living thing! And so in the midst of the wealth of food which Earth, the best of mothers, has produced, it is your pleasure to eat the piteous flesh of slaughtered animals.

> OVID
> *Metamorphoses*

I have no doubt that it is a part of the destiny of the human race, in its gradual improvement, to leave off eating animals, as surely as the savage tribes have left off eating each other when they come in contact with the more civilized.

> HENRY DAVID THOREAU
> *Walden*, 1854

Pure men like pure food which gives true health, balanced mentality, sustaining strength ... Pure food that promotes the knowledge of God.

> BHAGAVAD GITA

But man is a carnivorous production,
And must have meals, at least one meal a day; ...
Although his anatomical construction
Bears vegetables in a grumbling way,
Your labouring people think, beyond all question,
Beef, veal, and mutton, better for digestion.

> LORD BYRON
> *Don Juan*

It is a fact that great eaters of meat are in general more cruel and ferocious than other men; this observation holds good in all places and at all times; the barbarism of the English is well known.
>JEAN-JACQUES ROUSSEAU
>*Emile*

I have known many meat-eaters to be far more non-violent than vegetarians.
>MAHATMA GANDHI
>*Non-Violence in Peace and War*

Persons living entirely on vegetables are seldom of a plump and succulent habit.
>WILLIAM CULLEN
>*First Lines of the Practice of Physic*, 1778

Whether vegetarians are every guilty of excess in quantity, and eat to surfeit, I am not informed; but ... I find the food in general so to fill my stomach that it becomes painful to eat more the moment I have had enough.
>FRANCIS WILLIAM NEWMAN
>*Essays on Diet*, 1883

Vegetarianism is harmless enough, though it is apt to fill a man with wind and self-righteousness.
>SIR ROBERT HUTCHINSON

Tell me, have you eaten that or are you going to?
>attributed to J.M. BARRIE, seated at lunch next to Bernard Shaw and a plateful of greens

'You, a fervent vegetarian, tucking into rump-steak!'

'I'm steadfast as regards my principles. But Ethel's
thrown me over.'

Most vigitaryans I iver see looked enough like their food to be classes as cannybals.

> FINLEY PETER DUNNE
> *Mr Dooley's Philosophy*, 1900

I have no religious or moral objection to vegetables, but they are, as it were, dull. They are the also-rans of the plate.

> FRANK MUIR
> *You Can't Have Your Kayak and Heat It*

I'm very fond of pigs; but I don't find it difficult to eat them.

> ROBERT RUNCIE, Archbishop of Canterbury

I did not become a vegetarian for my health. I did it for the health of the chickens.

> ISAAC BASHEVIS SINGER

There is no disease, bodily or mental, which adoption of vegetable diet, and pure water has not infallibly mitigated, wherever the experiment has been fairly tried.

> PERCY BYSSHE SHELLEY
> *Queen Mab*

A cure of asthma. Live for a fortnight on boiled carrots only.

> JOHN WESLEY
> *Primitive Physic*, 1789.

Everything I eat has been proved by some doctor or other to be a deadly poison, and everything I don't eat has been proved to be indispensable for life.

> BERNARD SHAW

# *Short Commons*

There is poetry in a pork chop to a hungry man.
    PHILIP GIBBS
    *New York Times*, August 1951

We have water and polenta; let us rival Jove himself in happiness.
    SENECA
    *Epistulae ad Lucilium*

What a thing it is to sit down to dinner, after reading of the miseries in starving countries! One fancies one has no right to eat and drink.
    LEIGH HUNT
    *Table-Talk*, 1851

We sleek, well-fed folk can hardly realize what feeling hungry is like. We know what it is to have no appetite, and not to care for the dainty victuals placed before us, but we do not understand what it means to sicken for food – to die for bread while others waste it … Hunger is a luxury to us, a piquant, flavour-giving sauce. It is well worth while to get hungry and thirsty, merely to discover how much gratification can be obtained from eating and drinking. If you wish to thoroughly enjoy your dinner, take a thirty-mile country walk after breakfast, and don't touch anything till you get back.
    JEROME K. JEROME
    *The Idle Thoughts of an Idle Fellow*

The best bill of fare I know of is a good appetite.
    JOSH BILLINGS
    *His Works Complete*

41

The satisfaction of eating is so completely a matter of appetite that such distinction as there is between the luxurious and the hardy in regard to this enjoyment is altogether in favor of the hardy. Who does not remember some rough and perhaps scanty meal in camp, or on the march, or at sea, or in the woods, which was infinitely more delicious than the most luxurious dinner?

CHARLES W. ELIOT
*The Happy Life*, 1896

The boatswain of the ship did bring us out of the kettle a piece of hot salt beef, and some brown bread and brandy; and there we did make a little meal, but so good as I never would desire to eat better meat while I live, only I would have cleaner dishes.

SAMUEL PEPYS
*Diary*, 25 March 1669

From the shilling dinner of beef and carrots to the grandest banquets of the season – everything is good. There are no degrees in eating. I mean that mutton is as good as venison – beefsteak, if you are hungry, as good as turtle – bottled ale, if you like it, to the full as good as champagne; – there is no delicacy in the world which Monsieur Francatelli or Monsieur Soyer can produce, which I believe to be better than toasted cheese … You can but be hungry, and eat and be happy.

W.M. THACKERAY
*Travels in London*

Better is a dinner of herbs where love is than a fatted ox and hatred with it.

PROVERBS, 15:17

What a table was here spread for me in a wilderness,
where I saw nothing at first but to perish for hunger.
DANIEL DEFOE
*Robinson Crusoe*

'How shall we dine today?' is the first thought in
every rank of life, and of human beings everywhere.
ABRAHAM HAYWARD
*The Art of Dining*, 1852

The room in which the boys were fed, was a large stone hall, with a copper at one end: out of which the master, dressed in an apron for the purpose, and assisted by one or two women, ladled the gruel at meal-times. Of this festive composition each boy had one porringer, and no more – except on occasions of great public rejoicing, when he had two ounces and a quarter of bread besides. The bowls never wanted washing. The boys polished them with their spoons till they shone again.

CHARLES DICKENS
*Oliver Twist*

The best things beyond their measure cloy.

HOMER
*The Iliad*, translated by Alexander Pope

Mr Squeers had before him a small measure of coffee, a plate of hot toast, and a cold round of beef; but he was at that moment intent on preparing breakfast for the little boys.

'This is twopenn'orth of milk, is it, waiter?' said Mr Squeers, looking down into a large blue mug, and slanting it gently, so as to get an accurate view of the quantity of liquid contained in it.

'That's twopenn'orth, sir,' replied the waiter.

'What a rare article milk is, to be sure, in London!' said Mr Squeers with a sigh. 'Just fill that mug up with lukewarm water, William, will you?'

'To the wery top, sir?' inquired the waiter. 'Why, the milk will be drownded.'

'Never you mind that,' replied Mr Squeers. 'Serve it right for being so dear .... Conquer your passions, boys, and don't be eager after vittles.' As he uttered this moral precept, Mr Squeers took a large bite out of the cold beef.

CHARLES DICKENS
*Nicholas Nickleby*

44

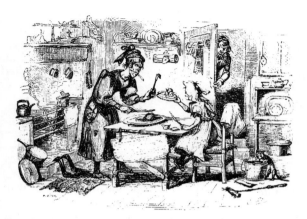

... an immense charger of broth, thickened with oatmeal and colewort, in which ocean of liquid was indistinctly discovered, by close observers, two or three short ribs of lean mutton sailing to and fro.

SIR WALTER SCOTT
*Old Mortality*
short commons at the Laird's table

The eye, can it feast when the stomach is starving?
Pray less of your gilding and more of your carving.
EGERTON WARBURTON
'On a Mean Host'

A growing, healthy lad, taking plenty of exercise, and careful to restrain himself from indulging in too much study, can generally satisfy the most exacting expectations as regards his feeding powers. It is amusing to see boys eat, when you have not got to pay for it. Their idea of a square meal is a pound and a half of roast beef with five or six good-sized potatoes ... plenty of greens, and four thick slices of

Yorkshire pudding, followed by a couple of currant dumplings, a few green apples, a pen' orth of nuts, half-a-dozen jumbles, and a bottle of ginger beer ...

But the boys have not all the advantages on their side. A boy never enjoys the luxury of being satisfied. A boy never feels full ... A dinner makes no difference whatever to a boy.

    JEROME K. JEROME
    *The Idle Thoughts of an Idle Fellow*

Popular fallacies: that enough is as good as a feast ... It is a vile cold-scrag-of-mutton sophism ... If nothing else could be said for a feast, this is sufficient, that from the superflux there is usually something left for the next day.

    CHARLES LAMB
    *The Essays of Elia*

Five muffins are enough for any man at any one meal, and the breast and wing of a chicken should suffice ... Very different, however, is the case of *pâté de foie gras*, sandwiches, oysters, and meringues. I cannot eat too many of these.

    E.V. KNOX
    *Gorgeous Times*

# Travellers' Fare

In reading the accounts of travellers who have suffered severely for want of food, a striking fact is common to all – that carrion and garbage of every kind can be eaten, under those circumstances, without the stomach rejecting it. And life can certainly be supported on a diet which would give severe illness to a man not driven to it by the pangs of hunger.

FRANCIS GALTON
*The Art of Travel*, 1854

When I cannot get a dinner to suit my taste I endeavor to get a taste to suit my dinner. I have made a hearty meal of Cucumbers & onions off of a dirty table in a filthy log hut on the banks of Black River and I have made as hearty a one in a vile French auberge of a stale fowl that I verily believe had mounted guard on the table a half score of times.

WASHINGTON IRVING
*Journal of a Tour Through France and Italy*,
10 September 1804

I opened a tin of Bologna sausage and broke a cake of chocolate, and that was all I had to eat. It may sound offensive, but I ate them together, bite by bite, by way of bread and meat. All I had to wash down this revolting mixture was neat brandy: a revolting beverage in itself. But I was rare and hungry; ate well, and smoked one of the best cigarettes in my experience.

ROBERT LOUIS STEVENSON
*Travels with a Donkey in the Cévennes*

We were astonished at its elegance in so desert a place ... Our supper consisted of two dishes of fine game, the one of heathcock, the other of woodcock, a creamy fresh butter, cheese of the country, a pot of preserved vaccinium [bilberries], a wild fruit which grows on the mountains, and port wine – all served up together. It was a luxurious repast for the country.

BARTHÉLÉMY FAUJAS DE ST FOND, the French Commissioner for wines, describing the inn at Dalmally in 1784
*Voyage en Angleterre*

'The finest landscape in the world is improved by a good inn in the foreground.

SAMUEL JOHNSON


'The coach stops here half an hour, gentlemen; dinner quite ready.'

'Tis a delightful sound. And what a dinner! What a profusion of substantial delicacies. What mighty and oris-tinted rounds of beef! What vast and marble-veined ribs! What gelatinous veal-pies! What colossal hams! Those are evidently prize cheese! And how invigorating is the perfume of those various and variegated pickles! Then the bustle emulating the plenty; the ringing of bells, the clash of thoroughfare, the summoning of ubiquitous waiters, and the all-pervading feeling of omnipotence from the guests, who order what they please to the landlord, who can produce and execute everything they can desire.

BENJAMIN DISRAELI


In front of a brilliant fire, a spit was turning, admirably covered with quails and those little corncrakes which are always so plump. This choice game was dripping over a huge roast ..., and on the side was a leveret, already cooked, the aroma of which would have embalmed a church. How splendid, I thought to myself, Providence hadn't altogether abandoned me. I asked the landlord ... what he was going to give me. 'Nothing but good food, monsieur; some good boiled meat, good potato soup, good shoulder of mutton and good beans.' At this unexpected answer, my high expectations were bitterly disappointed.

BRILLAT-SAVARIN
*La Physiologie du goût*

Why do they always put mud into coffee on board steamers? Why does the tea generally taste of boiled boots? Why is the milk scarce and thin? And why do they have those bleeding legs of boiled mutton for dinner? In the steamers of other nations you are well fed. Is it impossible that Britannia ... should attend to the victuals a little, and that meat should be well cooked under a Union Jack?

W. M. THACKERAY
*The Kickleburys on the Rhine*

It is a glorious thing to think that one is leaving France and all foreign kickshaws behind one, and is once more approaching dear honest old England, on the deck of a British steamer.

But let us come into the cabin and have a bit of breakfast before we get in.

Surely that table covered with a dirty sheet instead of a table-cloth is not prepared for our repast?

Why, this stale loaf must have been on board quite a week. It has evidently made several passages backwards and forwards in company with this extremely remarkable sample of butter.

Why does this coffee the Steward has just brought us look like ink and sawdust, and taste like something perplexing?

The Frenchman, who has been expecting *déjeuner à la fourchette*, is surveying with astonishment the dish of mutton-chops they have set down before him. It is a great pity that they are all two inches thick, and are underdone when cut.

I wonder whether he is thinking, as I am, of the clean, fresh, and trim restaurant table, the excellent *café au lait*, *petits-pains*, Normandy butter, and other 'foreign kickshaws' that he has just left behind him in France.

Though he has had to pay three shillings for his hot breakfast he has informed me that he will wait till he arrives, and take '*le lunch*' on shore.

I wonder whether he is aware that, if he makes this meal at the typical Refreshment-Room, he will have to content himself with stale sponge-cakes, the day-before-yesterday's buns, and small tins of lemon-drops.

A Dyspeptic Contributor to
*Punch*, October 1887

There is no beverage which is held in more universal esteem than good coffee, and none in this country at least, which is obtained with greater difficulty (unless indeed it be *pure* wine). We hear constant and well-founded complaints both from foreigners and English people, of the wretched compounds so commonly served up here under its name, especially in many lodging houses, hotels, and railway refreshment rooms; at some of the principal stations ... the coffee is too nauseous to be swallowed.

ELIZA ACTON
*Modern Cookery for Private Families*, 1845

The fare that awaits the weary, disconsolate traveller at English railway stations: the stodgy bun, Bath and penny varieties both, and the triangular sandwich; the tea drawn overnight, and the lukewarm bovril, hopelessly inadequate substitute for soup freshly made from beef or stock. At a luncheon bar thus wickedly equipped, eating becomes what it never should be! – a sad, terrible necessity, a pleasure-less safeguard against pangs of hunger.

ELIZABETH ROBINS PENNELL
*A Guide for the Greedy*, by a Greedy Woman, 1923

# British Food

The English are not very dainty and the greatest lords' tables, who do not keep French cooks, are covered only with large dishes of meat. They are strangers to bisks and pottage. Their pastry is coarse and ill-baked, their stewed fruits and confectionery ware cannot be eat.

SORBIÈRE, writing in 1663

Roast beef and mutton are all they have which is good. Heaven keep every Christian from their gravies ... And Heaven guard everyone from their naïve vegetables, which boiled away in water, are brought to the table just as God made them.

HEINRICH HEINE, on English cooking

The dinner of Englishmen, far more than of foreigners, implies a large joint of meat which has afterwards to be eaten cold. There is cold meat at breakfast, cold meat at luncheon, cold meat at supper, cold meat all the day – which is eaten with pickles for lack of good sauce.

E. S. DALLAS
*Kettner's Book of the Table*, 1877

Nothing but joints, joints, joints, sometimes, perhaps, a meat-pie, which, if you eat it, weighs upon your conscience, the idea that you have eaten the scraps of other people's dinners.

NATHANIEL HAWKINS

When I think of that huge round of parboiled ox-flesh, with sodden dumplings floating in a saline, greasy mixture, surrounded by carrots looking red with disgust and turnips pale with dismay, I cannot help a sort of inward shudder.

*Memoirs of a Stomach*, Written by Himself, 1853

The adage 'God sends meat and the devil sends cooks' must surely be of native parentage, for of no country is it so true as of our own. Perhaps had it not been for the influx among us of French and Italian experts we should not have progressed much beyond the pancake and oatmeal period.

W. CAREW HAZLITT
*Old Cookery Books and Ancient Cuisine*, 1886

What passes for cookery in England is an abomination (they agreed). It is putting cabbages in water. It is roasting meat till it is like leather. It is cutting off the delicious skins of vegetables.

VIRGINIA WOOLF
*To the Lighthouse*

Every country possesses, it seems, the sort of cuisine it deserves which is to say the sort of cuisine it is appreciative enough to want ... The English cook that way because that is the way they like it.

WAVERLEY ROOT
*The Food of France*

54

There was an odd smell in the passage, as if the concentrated essence of all the dinners that had been cooked in the kitchen since the house was built, lingered at the top of the kitchen stairs to that hour ... In particular, there was a sensation of cabbage; as if all the greens that had ever been boiled there, were evergreens.

CHARLES DICKENS
Mrs Todger's boarding-house, *Martin Chuzzlewit*

... cabbage bathed in Ye Olde Englyshe hot water, and rare Tudor trifle with plenty of lukewarm custard sauce.

RUTH MCKENNEY and RICHARD BRANSTEN
an American view of English food

Now for a chop house or coffee-room dinner! Oh, the 'orrible smell that greets you at the door! Compound of cabbage, pickled salmon, boiled beef, saw-dust, and anchovy sarce. 'Wot will you take, sir?' inquires the frowsy waiter, smoothin' the filthy cloth, 'soles, macrel, vitin's – werry good, boiled beef – nice cut, cabbage, weal and 'am, cold lamb and sallard.' – *Bah* the den's 'ot to suffocation – the kitchen's below – a trap door vomits up dinners in return for bellows down the pipe to the cook. Flies settle on your face – swarm on your head; a wasp travels round; everything tastes flat, stale, and unprofitable.

R.S. SURTEES
*Handley Cross*


I was forced to go to a blind chop-house, and dine for ten-pence upon gill-ale, bad broth, and three chops of mutton; and then go reeking from thence to the first minister of state.

JONATHAN SWIFT
*The Journal to Stella*


'Waiter,' said Bullfinch piteously, 'we have been a long time waiting.' The waiter who ought to wait upon us laid the blame upon the waiter who ought not to wait upon us, and said it was all that waiter's fault.

'We wish,' said Bullfinch, much depressed, 'to order a little dinner in an hour. What can we have?'

'What would you like to have, gentlemen?'...

We could have mock-turtle soup, a sole, curry, and roast duck. Agreed. At this table by this window. Punctually in an hour.

I had been feigning to look out of this window; but I had been taking note of the crumbs on all the tables, the dirty table-cloths, the stuffy, soupy, airless atmosphere, the stale leavings everywhere about, the deep gloom of the waiter who ought to wait upon us, and the stomach-ache with which a lonely traveller at a distant table in a corner was too evidently afflicted. I now pointed out to Bullfinch the alarming circumstance that this traveller had *dined*. We hurriedly debated whether, without infringement of good breeding, we could ask him to disclose if he had partaken of mock-turtle, sole, curry, or roast duck?

> CHARLES DICKENS
> *The Uncommercial Traveller*


There are two kinds of English cooking: good and average. Good English cooking is simply French cooking; average cooking in an average hotel for the average Englishman explains to a large extent the Englishman's bleakness and taciturnity.

> KAREL CAPEK


We have about half-a-dozen real English dishes, that exceed anything, in my opinion, to be met with in France; by English dishes I mean, a turbot and lobster sauce; ham and chicken; turtle; a haunch of venison; a turkey and oysters; and after these, there is an end of an English table.

> ARTHUR YOUNG
> *Travels in France*, 1792


... our barons of beef, our noble sirloins, our exquisite haunches, saddles, legs, and loins of Southdown mutton, our noble rounds of boiled beef, and those haunches of British venison, the envy and admiration of the world.

> JOSEPH BREGION and ANNE MILLER
> *The Practical Cook*, 1845

Old English fare I would define as being the very best native material, cooked in the plainest possible manner. We talk of English cookery, though it should really be termed British cookery, for Irish stew and Welsh lamb, Scotch beef and cock-a-leekie soup, and even a hagggis, can fairly be included.

LT.-COL. NATHANIEL NEWNHAM-DAVIS
*The Gourmet's Guide to London*, 1914

Do you know how we fare in this Scottish paradise? We make free with our landlord's mutton, which is excellent, his poultry-yard, his garden, his dairy, and his cellar, which are all well stored. We have delicious salmon, pike, trout, perch, par, etc, at the door, for the taking. The Firth of Clyde, on the other side of the hill, supplies us with mullet, red and grey, cod, mackerel, whiting, and a variety of sea-fish, including the finest herrings I ever tasted. We have sweet juicy beef, and tolerable veal, with delicate bread, from the little town of Dunbritton; and plenty of partridge, grouse, heath-cock, and other game.

TOBIAS SMOLLETT
*The Expedition of Humphry Clinker*

The cuisine is certainly a little queer, but he who, with a Connamara appetite, cannot enjoy Connamara fare, salmon, fresh from its lakes, eggs newly laid, excellent bread and butter, the maliest of potatoes ('laughing at you, and with their coats unbuttoned from the heat', but perhaps a trifle underboiled for our taste, until we learn to like them 'with a bone in them'), together with the best of whiskey, and our Burton beer; ... why he's not the man for Galway.

SAMUEL REYNOLDS HOLE
*A Little Tour in Ireland*, 1859

# French Cookery

France ... is a land of milk and honey, the best milk
and the most perfumed honey, where all the good
things of the earth overflow and are cooked to
perfection.

> WILLIAM BOLITHO
> *Camera Obscura*

When the Channel has been crossed you are in the
country of good soups, of good fowl, of good
vegetables, of good sweets, of good wine...

The British beef stands against all the world as the
meat noblest for the spit, though the French ox which
has worked its time in the fields gives the best
material for the soup-pot; and though the Welsh
lamb and the English sheep are the perfection of
mutton young and mutton old, the lamb nurtured on
milk till the hour of its death, and the sheep reared on
the salt-marshes of the north, make splendid
contribution to the Paris kitchens. Veal is practically
an unknown meat in London; and the calf which has
been fed on milk and yolk of egg, and which has flesh
as soft as a kiss and as white as snow, is only to be
found in the Parisian restaurants. Most of the good
restaurants in London import all their winged
creatures, except game, from France, and the Surrey
fowl and the Aylesbury duck, the representatives of
Great Britain, make no great show against the
champions of Gaul, though the Norfolk turkey holds
his own.

> LT.-COL. NATHANIEL NEWNHAM-DAVIS
> *The Gourmet's Guide to Europe*, 1903

In general France eats more consciously, more intelligently, than any other nation. It may be quails *financière*, or it may be a stew concocted from the rabbit that Papa Jacques caught yesterday under the hedge.

M.K. FISHER
*Serve It Forth*

The monotony of life in the provinces, and the lack of work, cause the mind to become preoccupied with cooking ... One does not dine as sumptuously as in Paris, but one dines better.

HONORÉ DE BALZAC

The cooking of Provence seems to me the best of all cooking; this is not said to hurt the feelings of other provinces, but because it is the truth.

MME LÉON DAUDET, 'Pampille'
*Les Bons Plats de France*, 1919

In the whole of French cooking there is no more evocative dish than *Soupe à l'oignon*, no dish better able to conjure up the sentimental, carefree feelings associated with unexpected nights of adventuring through the city streets.

ROBERT COURTINE
*Cent Merveilles de la cuisine française*

The official classes – and Nice is a great official city – the officers, the lawyers, the judges and the retired French bourgeois of the city, and the peasants from the hills on market day, see to it that they get inexpensively fed ... and tastefully! I will cite you a few *menus*. One I ate in the 'Boeuf à la Mode', in a back street ... Here I used to eat almost daily, ten years ago, at a cost of twelve francs fifty – then two shillings, or half a dollar ... Our fellow diners were all of the official or professional classes. We chose for hors d'oeuvres, *Salade Niçoise* and *Aubergines à la Turque*; grey – not red – mullet, grilled with a mustard-mixed-with-white-wine sauce; *poulet chasseur*; ices and fruit … Except for the ices everything was admirable … And French-admirable…

FORD MADOX FORD, writing in 1934
*Provence*

I spied from my window the sign of a Routier restaurant, which is to the Francophile English middle-class as a fine fat truffle is to a fine fat sow.

TOM VERNON
*Fat Man on a Bicycle*

# *Italian Cookery*

There is no cookery in Europe so often maligned without cause as that of Italy. People who are not sure of their facts often dismiss it as being 'all garlic and oil', whereas very little oil is used except at Genoa, where oil, and very good oil as a rule, takes the place of butter, and no more garlic than is necessary to give a slight flavour to the dishes in which it plays a part. An Italian cook frys better than one of any other nationality. In the north very good meat is obtainable, the boiled beef of Turin being almost equal to our own Silverside. Farther and farther south, as the climate becomes hotter, the meat becomes less and less the food of the people, various dishes of paste and fish taking its place, and as a compensation the fruit and the wine become more delicious. The fowls and figs of Tuscany, the white truffles of Piedmont, the artichokes of Rome, the walnuts and grapes of Sorrento, might well stir a gourmet to poetic flights.

LT.-COL. NATHANIEL NEWNHAM-DAVIS
*The Gourmet's Guide to Europe*, 1903

Catherine brought me up as a great treat yesterday at dinner, ham dressed with as much garlic as could be stewed into it, and a plate of raw figs, telling me I was to eat them together.

JOHN RUSKIN
in Assisi, July 1874

Maccaroni, a delicate, thoroughly-kneaded and cooked preparation of fine meal in various shapes, is to be got everywhere of all qualities for a trifle. It is cooked for the most part only in water, some pulverized cheese being added to lard and season the dish. At the corner of almost every large street you find pastry-cooks with their pans of hissing oil, especially on festival days, ready at any moment to prepare you fish and pastry to your taste. The confectioners have an incredible run of custom, many thousands of people carrying away from these open shops their dinners and suppers in pieces of paper.

> WOLFGANG GOETHE
> Fast food in Naples; *Travels in Italy*, 29 May 1787
> (translated by Revd A.J.W. Morrison, 1892)

It was very well cooked, but Mrs Fisher had never cared for maccaroni, especially not this long, worm-shaped variety. She found it difficult to eat – slippery, wriggling off her fork, making her look, she felt, undignified when, having got it as she supposed into her mouth, ends of it yet hung out … Francesca from the sideboard watched Mrs Fisher's way with maccaroni gloomily, and her gloom deepened when she saw her at last take her knife to it and chop it small. Mrs Fisher really did not know how else to get hold of the stuff.

> ELIZABETH VON ARNIM
> *The Enchanted April*

… he contrives, by some swiftly-adroit process of levitation, that the whole plateful shall rise in a noiseless and unbroken flood from the table to his mouth…

> NORMAN DOUGLAS, watching the consumption
> of a dish of maccaroni
> *Old Calabria*

No man is lonely while eating spaghetti.

> ROBERT MORLEY

63

There is no season of the year when you are not surrounded by edibles, and the Neapolitan desires not only the pleasure of eating, but also the gratification of his eye in the manner in which the wares are exposed for sale ... No shops are more choicely dressed than the butchers', which the people eye with special longing, the periodical abstinence to which they are subjected only serving to whet their carnivorous appetites.

You never see any pieces of beef, veal, or mutton hanging in the butchers' stalls without the fat of the flank or leg being profusely gilded. Different days of the year, in particular the Christmas holidays, are distinguished as days of feasting. There is then celebrated a universal Cocagna to which five hundred thousand persons have pledged their word ... The eye rests with extreme pleasure on the shops where green things are sold, where raisins, melons and figs are exposed. The eatables hang in garlands over the street; there you see huge paternosters of sausages laced with gold and red ribbons; Italian poultry all with red flags under their croups ... Besides these, a multitude of asses patrol the streets with green wares, with capons and lamb ... It is not enough, however, for the Neapolitans to consume all this. Every year a policeman goes the round of the whole town with a trumpeter, proclaiming at all squares and crossings, how many thousand oxen, calves, lambs, pigs, &c., the inhabitants have devoured. The people listen to the intelligence with the greatest interest, rejoicing immoderately at the huge figure, and each thinking with pleasure of the part he took in the consumption.

WOLFGANG GOETHE
*Travels in Italy*, 29 May 1787

I have observed a thing amongst the Venetians, ...
that their Gentlemen and greatest Senators ... will
come into the market, and buy their flesh, fish,
fruites, and such other things as are necessary for the
maintenance of their family: a token indeed of
frugality, which is commendable in all men; but me
thinkes it is not an argument of true generosity, that a
noble spirit should deject itself to these petty and
base matters, that are fitter to be done by servants.

> THOMAS CORYAT
> *Coryat's Crudities*, 1611

'Look! Look at the snow-white broccoli. Look at the
huge finocchi. Why don't we get them? I *must* have
some. Look at those great clusters of dates – ten
francs a kilo, and we pay sixteen.'

> D.H. LAWRENCE
> at the market in Palermo, *Sea and Sardinia*

In Ventimiglia ... the waiter with his Brooklyn accent
smiled ingratiatingly and said: 'We will cook-a you,
especialmente, a nice-a leetle slice of bleedin-a beef...'

> FORD MADOX FORD
> *Provence*

I have always liked highly seasoned, rich food, such
as macaroni prepared by a skilful Neapolitan cook, ...
game with a high flavour, and cheese which has
reached a state of perfection when the tiny organisms
making it up begin to come to life. And in women, I
have always found the odour of my beloved ones
exceedingly agreeable.

> GIACOMO CASANOVA
> *Memoirs*

# Round the World

There is no part of the world in which the connoisseur may not find some delicacy peculiar to the place – as the turkey, fattened on the olives of Mount Hymettus, at Athens; the famous *minestra del riso*, at Milan; the *pesce reale* (royal fish), at Naples; the *ombre chevalier* (a large species of char), of the lake of Geneva...

ABRAHAM HAYWARD
*The Art of Dining*

Then there is the beefsteak. They have it in Europe, but they don't know how to cook it. Neither will they cut it right ... It is a little overdone, is rather dry, it tastes pretty insipidly, it rouses no enthusiasm.

MARK TWAIN
*A Tramp Abroad*

The Portuguese had need have the stomach of ostriches to digest the loads of greasy victuals with which they cram themselves. Their vegetables, their rice, their poultry are all stewed in the essence of ham, and so strongly seasoned with pepper and spices that a spoonful of pease or a quarter of an onion is sufficient to set one's mouth in a flame. With such a diet ... I am not surprised at their complaining continually of headaches and vapours.

WILLIAM BECKFORD
*Travel Diaries*, 1787–88

The Spaniard, I have heard it said
Eats garlic, by itself, on bread...
HILAIRE BELLOC
*On Food*

The good Viennese pastries are already a thing of the past. Ah, yes, I say to myself, thinking of all this in my own house, having to eat a piece of quinquagenarian beef instead of delicious roast veal, a piece of yellowing mutton instead of a *ragoût aux croquettes*, a slice of roast leather instead of *faisan à la Bohémienne*, one of those stews called *Gross-Salat* instead of those excellent and delicately flavoured oranges, one of those dried apple puffs instead of those heavenly *pâtisseries*; ah, yes, I say to myself if only now I had a store of those pâtés which I could not eat in Vienna! Here at Esterház no one asks me, 'Would you like some chocolate? With or without milk? Or coffee, perhaps? Would you like an ice-cream? Vanilla or pineapple?'

JOSEPH HAYDN

in a letter to Marianne de Genzenger in 1780, following a stay with her in Vienna

*Englishmen abroad, as seen by* Punch *in 1875.*

Luxuriant diversity is a marked characteristic of American cookery ... No nation possesses so wide a field for administering to its most minute wants at all seasons and under all conditions. The woods, the waters, and the plains vie with one another in their contributions to the table. If we have not the truffle, we have the mushroom. If we are without the turbot and sole, we have the whitefish, the shad, the flounder, the bluefish, the striped-bass, the frost-fish and pompano – the choice from ice-cold to tropical waters, the range from the Atlantic to the Pacific – with oysters unequalled in delicacy and cheapness.

> GEORGE ELLWANGER
> *The Pleasures of the Table*, 1903

The sole are not quite as good as Dover sole; but you can get better lobsters in New York than anywhere in the world, and deep-sea oysters, too.

> FRANK HARRIS
> *My Life and Loves*

Receptive and creative, America has learned from all, and added to acquired knowledge the results of her own inventive genius ... An American dinner has come to be recognized as among the very best it is possible to obtain.

> GEORGE ELLWANGER
> *The Pleasures of the Table*, 1903

Americans can eat garbage, provided you sprinkle it liberally with ketchup, mustard, chili sauce, tobasco sauce, cayenne pepper, or any other condiment which destroys the original flavor of the dish.

> HENRY MILLER
> *Remember to Remember*

*'What will you have to follow, Sir?'* American
diner (faced with tough looking steak):
*'Indigestion, I guess.'*

An American always knows what he wants, asks for
it, and keeps on asking until he gets it.
>LT.-COL. NATHANIEL NEWNHAM-DAVIS
>*The Gourmet's Guide to London*, 1914

Of course meat is the staple of Australian life. A working-man whose family did not eat meat three times a day would indeed be a phenomenon. High and low, rich and poor, all eat meat to an incredible extent, even in the hottest weather.

RICHARD TWOPENY
*Town Life in Australia*, 1883

On Monday we've mutton with damper and tea;
On Tuesdays, tea, damper and mutton…
FRANCIS LANCELOTT
'On Monday We've Mutton', c. 1852

The mightly pavlova, dripping with passionfruit and topped with mountainous swirls of crusted meringue, may set tastebuds of Australian youth watering, but it has never had the gourmets of Paris besieging the doors of the Australian embassy, begging for the recipe.

*Weekend Australian*, 1985

France and China are the only two countries that have both cuisine and courtesy.

CURNONSKY

The Russians are a nation of gourmands, for the *Zakouska*, the potatoes and celery, spiced eels, stuffed crayfish, chillies stuffed with potato, olives, minced red cabbage, smoked goose-flesh, smoked salmon, smoked sturgeon, raw herring, pickled mushrooms, radishes, caviar, and a score of other 'appetisers', and the *petits patés*, the *Rastegai* (tiny pies of the lightest paste with a complicated fish stuffing and a little fresh caviar in the openings at the top), … could only be consumed by vigorous eaters. Soups are the contribution of Russia to the cuisine of the world, and the moujik, when he first stirred some sour cream into his cabbage broth, little thought that from his raw idea the majestic Bortch would come into existence.

LT.-COL. NATHANIEL NEWNHAM-DAVIS
*The Gourmet's Guide to Europe,* 1903


Many a bad dinner I made from the mere fatigue of being offered fifty or sixty different dishes by servants who come one after the other and flourish ready carv'd fish, flesh, fowl, Vegetables, fruits, soups of fish, etc., before your eyes, wines, Liqueures, etc., in their turn. Seriously the profusion is beyond anything I ever saw.

MARTHA and CATHERINE WILMOT
a Moscow dinner in 1804, *Russian Journals*


'Well now, my friend, give us two – or better still, three dozen oysters, vegetable soup…'

'*Printanière*,' interjected the Tatar waiter. But Stepan Arkadyich visibly did not wish to give him the satisfaction of calling the dishes by their French names.

'With vegetables in it, know the one? Then turbot with a really thick sauce, followed by … roast beef; and see that it's good. Maybe capons after that, and then preserves.'

The Tatar, recalling that it was Stepan Arkadyich's way not to call the dishes by their names on the French menu, did not repeat the order after him, but gave himself the pleasure of using the French words: '*Soupe printanière, turbot sauce Beaumarchais, poularde à l'estragon, macédoine de fruits…*'

LEO TOLSTOY
Oblonsky dines with Levin, *Anna Karenina*

71

'Prison cuisine is to be improved. The chefs, who are nominally warders in the several prisons, are to undergo a course of training in cookery at Wormwood Scrubs.' – Daily Telegraph, *October 1899*

*Prisoner*: This 'ere is all very well, but I likes to know what I'm eating!' (old *Punch* cartoon)

Many gastronomic expressions and names of dishes
... would lose their piquancy or precise colouring on
translation ... *'Les quenelles de levraut saucées d'une
espagnolle au fumet'*, *'les amourettes de boeuf marinées
frites'*, *'l'épaule de veau en musette champêtre'*, *'un coq
vierge en petit deuil'*, ... while natural and comprehen-
sible in French, would sound somewhat bizarre as
'Forcemeat balls of leverets sauced with a racy
Spanish woman', 'the love-affairs of soused beef
fried', 'a shoulder of veal in rural bagpipes', and 'a
virgin rooster in half-mourning'.

> GEORGE H. ELLWANGER
> *The Pleasures of the Table*, 1903

*Dyspeptic diner* (forking the food suspiciously): 'What
is it, waiter?'
*Waiter*: 'It says "Ronyongs Sorty" on the menoo, Sir,
but I can't say what it may be on the dish!'

> caption to 1882 *Punch* cartoon

In the whole range of literature and science, there is
nothing to be found comparable to the inaccuracy
and corruption of culinary language.

> E.S. DALLAS
> *Kettner's Book of the Table*, 1877

Every good cook has his little vanities. They are all
inventors; and when any one of them, breaking away
from the strict lines of the classic *haute cuisine*, finds
that a pinch of this or two drops of that improves
some well-known dish, he immediately gives it a new
name.

> LT.-COL. NATHANIEL NEWNHAM-DAVIS
> *Dinners and Diners*, 1899

VENDØME

*Restaurant*

→ MENU →

# Eating Out

He ordered as one to the menu born.
> O. HENRY

It takes much art
To choose à la carte
For less than they quote
For the table d'hôte.
> JUSTIN RICHARDSON
> *La Carte*

I lunched at the Rainbow, a type of City restaurant which is passing away. A large dark room, sombrely furnished in mahogany, and gaslighted, even in the sunshine of a hot July day. In the centre a table at which a stout carver in white cap, coat and apron, carves the saddle of mutton and the sirloin of beef – dishes which are never varied, and of which the customers never seem to tire. Here come lawyers and other *hommes d'affaires* of middle-age to whom luncheon is a serious meal, not to be ordered without minute instructions to the obsequious waiter. 'Do you call this underdone?' a portly customer asks sharply. 'Yes, sir.' 'Well, I don't. Take it back.' 'Yes, sir.' Here one drinks either stout from a tankard, or some sound wine; but if one orders wine, one gives the waiter directions as to the temperature. It is *de rigueur*. The door leading into the dining-room is labelled 'coffee room', and there is a significant notice 'Ladies' dining room upstairs'.

> ARNOLD BENNETT
> *Journals*, 13 July 1897

44 today. Yesterday for a change we lunched alone and dined alone. Dined at Savoy Grill Room. The only good service I have come across this time in London, outside clubs.

> ARNOLD BENNETT
> *Journals*, 27 May 1911

... like an airport lounge and the longest wait between courses I can remember.

> MICHAEL WINNER of one of London's top hotels
> *Sunday Times*, 6 June 1993

*Diner*: I'd complain about the service if I could find a waiter to complain to.
  MEL CALMAN
  caption to cartoon, 1971

Memo to meek diners: bellow for better service.
  MICHAEL WINNER
  *Sunday Times*, 6 June 1993

The best method, which I use a great deal, is to raise my napkin in the air, arm outstretched above the head, and wave it around slowly. That always gets them.
  MICHAEL WINNER
  *Sunday Times*, 30 May 1993

I have been saucily bespattered in some of London's leading hotels ... It is a sin one never forgives.
ROBIN YOUNG
*The Times*, 8 May 1993

When going to an eating house, go to one that is filled with customers.
CHINESE PROVERB

It was in a restaurant that was once one of the Meccas for the mixed gourmets of the world. We overlooked the Mediterranean and the ghosts of grand dukes, famous beauties, forgotten geniuses, and famous rastas lurked in the shadows of the less lit colonnades. We had *Potage Grand Duc Alexandre; Turbot Poché Princess de Galles, Sauce Escoffier*. We had *Civet de Lièvre à la Reine d'Angleterre*, the usual chicken with salad *des Quatre Saisons, pêche Melba, Petites Friandises Meyerbeer, Fromages Assortis*. It sounds good, doesn't it?...

My lovely English friends expressed themselves ravished and drove off into the blue night, romantically, along the Corniche. When we had done waving handkerchiefs we retired hastily to a solitary spot beside the Casino and ... shot our lunches ... We were neither of us up to food for several days.

The *Potage Grand Duc Alexandre* had been tepid, greenish, bill-sticker's paste; the *Turbot Poché Princesse de Galles*, tepid white blotting-paper drenched with white bill-sticker's paste; Queen Victoria's jugged hare had been tepid, black-brown dough drenched with mahogany-brown bill-sticker's paste; ... the *pêche Melba* had been a gummy substance from a Californian can drenched with tepid, pink, bill-sticker's paste.

> FORD MADOX FORD
> *Provence*


All yesterday I was ill – probably owing to mussel-soup at Sylvain's on Monday night, but I do not feel sure.

> ARNOLD BENNETT
> *Journals*, 6 January 1904


All I ask of food is that it doesn't harm me.

> MICHAEL PALIN

Yesterday when I was in Paillard's, it occurred to me that the difference between the most excessively *chic* restaurant and an ordinary good one is very slight. Paillard's has the reputation of being the best, or one of the three best in Paris, and therefore in the world. Yet it is small, and not in the least luxurious, and the waiting is no better than it is elsewhere ... The food was very good, and so was the wine. But scarcely appreciably better than at Sylvain's, Maire's, or Noel and Peters. And the prices were about twenty-five per cent dearer than at those other places – not more.

In the evening, at a Boulant, I had for 6*d*. a bifteck and soufflé potatoes better than which could not possibly be obtained anywhere, at no matter what price. When you have thoroughly good, well-flavoured, tender meat, perfectly cooked, – you cannot surpass that.

ARNOLD BENNETT
*Journals,* 27 April 1904


Today I was dining at Voisin's for twelve francs as usual, and I continue to marvel at having, for that price, first rate meat, vegetables done in butter rather than margarine, and a half bottle of very drinkable wine. I heard that lunches cost thirty or fifty francs a head at the restaurant that has opened in La Paiva's house [a courtesan, friend of Goncourt], and when I asked what one could possibly have to justify that price, all I could get out of anyone was 'Caviar ... caviar such as you can't get anywhere else!' You can keep the caviar – I'm quite content with my simple French meal.

EDMOND DE GONCOURT
*Journal,* 9 May 1895

Around the tables the waiters in their white aprons
and the *maîtres d'hôtel* and the silver-chained
*sommeliers* moved noiselessly, and the master-spirit of
the whole, M. Ritz, ... with his hands clasped
nervously ... went from table to table with a carefully
graduated scale of acknowledgment of the patrons ...
The fish, a fish-pie, with its macaroni and shrimps,
was delicious, and then came the triumph of the
dinner. Cased in its jelly covering, served on a great
block of ice, melting like snow in the mouth, Maître
Escoffier's *mousse* was an absolute masterpiece. The
*poulet*, too, was as good to eat as it had sounded when
M. Echenard (the manager) had described it to me,
and the *parfait de foie gras* was another delight. The
asparagus and the ice were but the trifles of the
dinner; but the ice swan that bore the little mock
peaches was a very graceful piece of table decoration.

LT.-COL. NATHANIEL NEWNHAM-DAVIS, dining at
the Savoy when César Ritz and Auguste
Escoffier were working there
*Dinners and Diners*, 1899

When Jones minor had made a clean sweep of the plate of *petits fours*, and had drained the last drops of his glass of Chartreuse, I thought I might venture to ask him how he liked his dinner as a whole ... He had drunk a glass of Amontillado, a glass of '89 Liebfraumilch, two glasses of Deutz and Gelderman, a glass of dessert claret, and a glass of liqueur, and when pressed for a critical opinion, said that he thought that it was jolly good.

> LT.-COL. NATHANIEL NEWNHAM-DAVIS
> *The Gourmet's Guide to London*, 1914, describing
> how he dined a Harrow schoolboy at the
> Trocadero in London

When *Paté de Foie Gras* becomes a horror, truffles a burden, and rich sauces an abomination, I go to one of the Tavernes ... and order the simplest and least greasy soup on the bill of fare, some plainly grilled cutlets, and some green vegetables. A pint of the second or third claret on the wine-card washes down this penitential repast.

> LT.-COL. NATHANIEL NEWNHAM-DAVIS
> *The Gourmet's Guide to Europe*, 1903

Great restaurants are, of course, nothing but mouth-brothels. There is no point in going to them if one intends to keep one's belt buckled.

> FREDERIC RAPHAEL
> *Sunday Times* Magazine, September 1977

We look for more than breast of quail
Served up with three snow peas ...

> BARBARA ABELL on nouvelle cuisine
> *Melbourne Living*, 1985

# In the Kitchen

Whoever writes a new book on cookery has to begin with an apology – there are so many, and most of them so bad. All contain good ideas, original or borrowed; but most of them are chaotic and overlaid with rubbish – the wildest confusion of receipts, distinctions without differences, and endless repetitions – the result of stupidity, of vanity, and of slavish deference to authority. A trifling variation is given to a well-known dish; a new name is bestowed upon it to flatter somebody's vanity; and then follows another and another receipt to choke up the cookery books and to bewilder their readers.

E.S. DALLAS
*Kettner's Book of the Table*, 1877

The world stands much less in need of additional inventions ... than of an expert anthologist to garner the most worthy among recipes already existing in such bewildering profusion.

GEORGE H. ELLWANGER
*The Pleasure of the Table*, 1903

The Author has submitted to a labour no preceding Cookery-Book-Maker, perhaps, ever attempted to encounter, – having *eaten* each Receipt before he set it down in his book.

I did not presume to offer any observations of my own, till I had read all that I could find written on the subject ... These books vary very little from each other ... equally unintelligible to those who are ignorant, and useless to those who are acquainted with the business of the Kitchen.

During the Herculean labour of my tedious

progress through these books, few of which afford the germ of a single idea, I have often wished that the authors of them had been satisfied with giving us the results of their own practice and experience – instead of idly perpetuating the errors, prejudices, and plagiarisms of their predecessors.

DR WILLIAM KITCHINER
*The Cook's Oracle*, 1821


Very many people at present seem to think, that, if they do but buy a cookery-book, they are providing a talisman which should make all things possible to any *chef de cuisine* who can read it.

A cookery-book, however, can no more make a cook, than a shilling handbook of oil-painting can make a Sir Joshua Reynolds. Some previous practical acquaintance with cookery as a manual art is needed to make even its language intelligible.

M.M. MALLOCK
*A Younger Sons' Cookery Book*, 1896


*Cookery, n.* A household art and practice of making unpalatable that which was already indigestible.

AMBROSE BIERCE
*The Enlarged Devil's Dictionary*


And now with some pleasure I find that it's seven; and must cook dinner. Haddock and sausage meat. I think it is true that one gains a certain hold on sausage and haddock by writing them down.

VIRGINIA WOOLF
*A Writer's Diary*

Who would suppose, from Adam's simple ration,
That cookery could have call'd forth such
resources,
As form a science and a nomenclature
From out the commonest demands of nature?
  LORD BYRON

Cooking is an art, and so is eating. If we don't know how to cook, we're not likely to know how to eat.

JOHN ERSKINE
*The Complete Life*

If one has the art, then a piece of celery or salted cabbage can be made into a marvellous delicacy; whereas if one has not the art, not all the greatest delicacies and rarities of land, sea or sky are of any avail.

YUAN MEI
*Poems* (translated by Arthur Waley, 1956)

On the tray there were liqueurs and herb brandy, mushrooms, rye flour biscuits made with buttermilk, comb honey, frothy mead, apples, and nuts both raw and roasted or preserved in honey. Then Anisya Fyodorovna brought in more preserves made with honey and sugar, ham, and a just roasted chicken. And all these delicacies, which she had made herself, seemed to smell and taste, as it were, of her. All had something of her white, pristine, plump figure and warm smile.

LEO TOLSTOY
*War and Peace*

Forty pounds might be lavished on a dinner which would make an epicure say that every dish was detestable; whilst a tenth part of the sum, employed with discrimination and skill, would provide one which every epicure would pronounce to be in its own way perfect.

Perfection, however, in cookery, depends, beyond anything else, on a complete knowledge of one's own limitations.

M.M. MALLOCK
*A Younger Sons' Cookery Book*, 1896

One only eats well at home.
FRENCH SAYING

# Grace

Some people have food, but no appetite; others have an appetite, but no food. I have both. The Lord be praised.

    grace attributed to OLIVER CROMWELL


Some hae meat and canna eat,
And some wad eat that want it,
But we hae meat and we can eat,
And sae the Lord be thankit.
    ROBERT BURNS
    'The Selkirk Grace'


Mr Pecksniff said grace: a short and pious grace, invoking a blessing on the appetites of those present, and committing all persons who had nothing to eat, to the care of Providence; whose business (so said the grace, in effect) it clearly was, to look after them.

    CHARLES DICKENS
    *Martin Chuzzlewit*


When I have sat at rich men's tables, with the savoury soup and messes steaming up the nostrils and moistening the lips of the guests with desire and a distracted choice, I have felt that the introduction of that ceremony (Grace) to be unreasonable. With the ravenous orgasm upon you, it seems impertinent to interpose a religious sentiment. It is a confusion of purpose to mutter out praises from a mouth that waters.

    CHARLES LAMB
    'Dissertation on Roast Pig', *Essays of Elia*

Does any man of common sense
Think ham and eggs give God offence?
Or that herring has a charm
The Almighty's anger to disarm?
Wrapped in His majesty divine,
D'you think He cares on what we dine?
JONATHAN SWIFT
'No Grace Before Meat'


One ought to be grateful, I quite apprehend,
Having dinner and supper and plenty to spend.
And so, suppose now, while the things go away,
By way of a grace we all stand up and say,
How pleasant it is to have money, heigh-ho!
How pleasant it is to have money!
ARTHUR HUGH CLOUGH
'Le Dîner', from *Dipsychus*, 1865

91

# Breakfast

The morning cup of coffee has an exhilaration about it which the cheering influence of the afternoon or evening cup of tea cannot be expected to reproduce.

    OLIVER WENDELL HOLMES
    *Over the Teacups*

A meagre, unsubstantial breakfast causes a sinking sensation of the stomach and bowels. Robert Browning truly remarks that

  'A sinking at the lower abdomen
  Begins the day with indifferent omen.'

    PYE HENRY CHAVASSE
    *Advice to a Wife*

He that would eat a good dinner, let him eat a good breakfast.

> JOHN RAY
> *English Proverbs*, 1678

I don't as a general thing become what you might call breakfast-conscious till I've had my morning tea and rather thought things over a bit.

> P.G. WODEHOUSE
> *Thank You, Jeeves*

Dick was about to answer that he felt much better, though still as weak as need be, when his little nurse ... set his breakfast before him, and insisted on his taking it before he underwent the fatigue of speaking or of being spoken to. Mr Swiveller, who was perfectly ravenous, and had had, all night, amazingly distinct and consistent dreams of mutton chops, double stout, and similar delicacies, felt even the weak tea and dry toast such irresistible temptations, that he consented to eat and drink upon one condition.

> CHARLES DICKENS
> *The Old Curiosity Shop*

We will not speak of all Queequeg's peculiarities here; how he eschewed coffee and hot rolls, and applied his undivided attention to beefsteaks, done rare.

> HERMAN MELVILLE
> *Moby Dick*

I went yesterday ... to breakfast with the Duke de Broglie. There was no cloth upon the table ... There was roast fowl, spinach, eggs, apples, wine, and afterwards they brought tea.

> REVD SYDNEY SMITH

Our breakfast consisted of what the Squire denominated true old English fare. He indulged in some bitter lamentations over modern breakfasts of tea-and-toast, which he censured as among the causes of modern effeminacy and weak nerves, and the decline of old English heartiness; and though he admitted them to his table to suit the palates of his guests, yet there was a brave display of cold meats, wine and ale, on the sideboard.

WASHINGTON IRVING
*Old Christmas*


The divine took his seat at the breakfast-table, and began to compose his spirits by the gentle sedative of a large cup of tea, the demulcent of a well buttered muffin, and the tonic of a small lobster.

*The Rev. Dr Folliott*: You are a man of taste, Mr Crotchet. A man of taste is seen at once in the array of his breakfast-table … Chocolate, coffee, tea, cream, eggs, ham, tongue, cold fowl – all these are good, and bespeak good knowledge in him who sets them forth: but the touchstone is fish: anchovy is the first step, prawns and shrimps the second; and I laud him who reaches even to these: potted char and lampreys are the third, and a fine stretch of progression; but lobster is, indeed, matter for a May morning, and demands a rare combination of knowledge, and virtue in him who sets it forth.

THOMAS LOVE PEACOCK
*Crotchet Castle*


'Now we'll commence,' said Adrian, tapping his egg with meditative cheerfulness; but his expression soon changed to one of pain, all the more alarming for his benevolent efforts to conceal it. Could it be possible the egg was bad? oh, horror! Lucy watched him, and waited in trepidation.

'This egg has boiled three minutes and three-quarters,' he observed, ceasing to contemplate it.

'Dear, dear!' said Lucy, 'I boiled them myself exactly that time. Richard likes them so. And you like them hard, Mr Harley?'

'On the contrary, I like them soft. Two minutes and a half, or three-quarters at the outside. An egg should never rashly verge upon hardness – never. Three minutes is the excess of temerity.'

> GEORGE MEREDITH
> *The Ordeal of Richard Feverel*

*'I'm afraid you've got a bad egg, Mr Jones!'*
The Curate: *'Oh no, my Lord, I assure you! Parts of it are excellent!' From* Punch *in 1895.*

The quality of eggs depends much upon the food given to the hen.

> ISABELLA BEETON
> *Book of Household Management*, 1861

'Mrs Bates, let me propose your venturing on one of these eggs. An egg boiled very soft is not unwholesome. Serle understands boiling an egg better than anybody. I would not recommend an egg boiled by anybody else – but you need not be afraid, they are very small, you see – one of our small eggs will not hurt you.'

JANE AUSTEN
*Emma*


The hymn 'Onward Christian Soldiers', sung to the right tune and in a not-too-brisk tempo, makes a very good egg timer. If you put the egg into boiling water and sing all five verses and chorus, the egg will be just right when you come to Amen.

a letter in the *Daily Telegraph*, 1983


Harris proposed that we should have scrambled eggs for breakfast. He said he would cook them. It seemed, from his account, that he was very good at doing scrambled eggs. He often did them at picnics and when out on yachts. He was quite famous for them.

The result was not altogether the success that Harris had anticipated. There seemed so little to show for the business. Six eggs had gone into the frying-pan, and all that came out was a teaspoonful of burnt and unappetizing-looking mess.

JEROME K. JEROME
*Three Men in a Boat*


No bacon anywhere else in the world is as good as that which the kitchenmaids fry in thousands of British kitchens.

LT.-COL. NATHANIEL NEWNHAM-DAVIS
*The Gourmet's Guide to London*, 1914

96

''Tis but simple fare,' said Coningsby, as the maiden uncovered the still hissing bacon and the eggs, that looked like tufts of primroses.

'Nay, a national dish,' said the stranger, glancing quickly at the table, 'whose fame is a proverb. And what more should we expect under a simple roof! How much better than an omelette or a greasy olla, that they would give us in a posada! 'Tis a wonderful country this England!

BENJAMIN DISRAELI
*Coningsby*


... greasy bacon and lacquered eggs, and coffee composed of frigid dregs.

OGDEN NASH of English hotel breakfasts


Bacon is not good for them that have weak stomacks: for it is of hard digestion, and breedeth cholerick humors. But for strong labouring men, and them that have good stomacks, it is convenient enough.

TOBIAS VENNER
*Via Recta ad Vitam Longam*, 1620


A Highland breakfast: One kit of boiled eggs; a second, full of butter; a third, full of cream; an entire cheese made of goat's milk; a large earthen pot, full of honey; the best part of a ham; a cold venison pastry; a bushel of oatmeal, made into thin cakes and bannocks, with a small wheaten loaf in the middle, for the strangers; a stone bottle full of whiskey, another of brandy, and a kilderkin of ale ... Great justice was done to the collation by the guests.

TOBIAS SMOLLETT
*Humphrey Clinker*

Our breakfasts are a disgrace to England. One would think the whole nation was upon a regimen of tea and toast – from the Land's End to Berwick-upon-Tweed, nothing but tea and toast – Your Ladyship must really acknowledge the prodigious advantage the Scotch possess over us in that respect ... The breakfasts! that's what redeems the land ...

SUSAN FERRIER
*Marriage*

... a dram of whisky, gin, rum or brandy, plain or infused with berries that grow among the heath; French rolls, oat and barley bread; tea and coffee; honey in the comb, red and black-currant jellies; marmalade, conserves and excellent cream; fine-flavoured butter, fresh and salted; Cheshire and Highland cheese, the last very indifferent; a plateful of very fresh eggs; fresh and salted herrings broiled; ... cold round of venison, beef and mutton hams.

JOHN KNOX
*A Tour Through the Highlands of Scotland*, 1776

'Do they really eat so much?' asked Fräulein Stiegelauer. 'Soup and baker's bread and pig's flesh, and tea and coffee and stewed fruit, and honey and eggs, and cold fish and kidneys, and hot fish and liver? All the ladies eat too?'

KATHERINE MANSFIELD
*In a German Pension*

Continental breakfasts are very sparse, usually just a pot of coffee or tea and a teensy roll ... My advice is to go right to lunch without pausing.

MISS PIGGY
*Miss Piggy's Guide to Life*, 1981

# Lunch

To dine well, authorities have proclaimed in *ex cathedra* utterance, you must lunch lightly; but not, therefore, does it follow that the light luncheon should be repellently prosaic. Let it be dainty – a graceful lyric – that it may fill you with hope of the coming dinner.

ELIZABETH ROBINS PENNELL
*A Guide for the Greedy,* by a Greedy Woman, 1923

I had had some literary business to transact with a great publishing firm somewhere near the bottom of Broadway, and my interview with them had not been of a very pleasant nature ... There were three partners, but at the outset I only saw two of them. One was a very methodical gentleman, bristling all over with figures; the other seemed to be of somewhat a theological tendency; but I could not make, in the way of business, anything satisfactory of either. I left the office in dudgeon, and was wending my way up Broadway ... when I heard a quick step behind me. A hand was laid on my arm, and I was accosted by a little stout gentleman, who introduced himself to me in the friendliest imaginable manner. 'You didn't get along very well with our people,' he remarked. 'You have seen the arithmetical partner and the pious one; I, sir, am the festive partner! Oysters on the half-shell, and Heidsieck's dry Monopole, white seal, at Delmonico's at once.' And, through the agency of the 'festive' partner, I made a very satisfactory business arangement with the house.

GEORGE AUGUSTUS SALA
*The Thorough Good Cook,* 1895

The lunch on this occasion began with soles, sunk in a deep dish, over which the college cook had spread a counterpane of the whitest cream, save that it was branded here and there with brown spots like the spots on the flanks of a doe. After that came the partridges, but if this suggests a couple of bald, brown birds on a plate you are mistaken. The partridges, many and various, came with all their retinue of sauces and salads, the sharp and the sweet, each in its order; their potatoes, thin as coins but not so hard; their sprouts, foliated as rosebuds but more succulent. And no sooner had the roast and its retinue been done with than the silent serving-man, ... set before us, wreathed in napkins, a confection which rose all sugar from the waves. To call it pudding and so relate it to rice and tapioca would be an insult. Meanwhile the wineglasses had flushed yellow and flushed crimson; had been emptied; had been filled.

VIRGINIA WOOLF
*A Room of One's Own*

I lunched at my usual restaurant where I am expected, and where my maternal waitress advised me in the selection of my lunch.

ARNOLD BENNETT
*Journals*, 11 November 1903

Lunched at the Golden Egg. Oh, the horror – the cold stuffiness, claustrophobic placing of tables, garish lights and mass produced food in steel dishes. And the egg-shaped menu!

BARBARA PYM
*Diary*, 27 November 1964

# Picnics

A picnic should be held among green things. Green turf is absolutely essential. There should be trees, broken ground, small paths, thickets, and hidden recesses ... Above all, there should be running water.
ANTHONY TROLLOPE
*Can You Forgive Her?*

There, on a slope of orchard, Francis laid
A damask napkin wrought with horse and hound,
Brought out a dusky loaf that smelt of home,
And, half-cut-down, a pasty costly-made,
Where quail and pigeon, lark and leveret lay,
Like fossils of the rock, with golden yolks
Imbedded and injellied ...
ALFRED, LORD TENNYSON
'Audley Court'

Soon each carriage disgorges marvellous delicacies from Perigord and Strasbourg, and other portable good things ... Nor has champagne been forgotten ... Seating themselves on the grass, they eat while the corks fly and glasses sparkle. There is talking, laughter and lively wit, for the world is their dining-room and the sun their lamp. And appetite, Nature's special gift, lends the meal a vivacity unknown indoors.

BRILLAT-SAVARIN
*La Physiologie du goût*

Captain Bellfield and Mrs Greenhow constantly had their heads together in the same hamper. I by no means intend to insinuate that there was anything wrong in this. People engaged in unpacking pies and cold chicken must have their hands in the same hamper.

ANTHONY TROLLOPE
*Can You Forgive Her?*

'A table spread in the shade, you know. Everything as natural and simple as possible. Is not that your idea?'

'Not quite. My idea of the simple and the natural will be to have the table spread in the dining-room. The nature and the simplicity of gentlemen and ladies, with their servants and furniture, I think is best observed by meals within doors.'

> JANE AUSTEN
> *Emma*

We hold that a picnic is not a picnic where there are well arranged tables and footmen to wait. It is merely an uncomfortable out of doors dinner. A picnic should entail a little of the trouble and enterprise of life, gathering sticks, lighting the fire, boiling the pot, buying or stealing potatoes.

> R.S. SURTEES
> *Plain and Ringlets*

Twenty minutes passed, during which the gentlemen stood round the fire staring at the pot, while the ladies got flowery wreaths and green and wild roses to adorn the dishes and table cloth spread under an oak tree and covered with provisions. Then the pot hook was adjusted, the pot heaved and swung off the fire, a fork plunged into the potatoes and they were triumphantly pronounced to be done to a turn. Then there was a dispute how they should be treated. 'Pour away the water,' said one. 'Let the water stay in the pot', said another. 'Steam the potatoes', 'Pour them out on the ground', 'Hand them round in the pot', 'Put them on a plate', 'Fish them out with a fork'. They were, however, poured out on the ground and then the pot fell upon them, crushing some and blackening others. Eventually the potatoes were handed round the table cloth, every one being most assiduous and urgent in recommending and passing them to his neighbour.

REVD FRANCIS KILVERT
*Diary*, 21 June 1870, a picnic at Snodhill

'And here's a mouthful of bread and bacon that mis'ess have sent, shepherd. The cider will go down better with a bit of victuals. Don't ye chaw quite close, shepherd, for I let the bacon fall in the road outside as I was bringing it along, and may be 'tis rather gritty. There, 'tis clane dirt; and we all know what that is ... Don't let your teeth quite meet, and you won't feel the sandiness at all.'

THOMAS HARDY
*Far from the Madding Crowd*
Gabriel Oak's sandy bacon sandwich.

With dispatchful looks in haste
She turns, on hospitable thoughts intent,
What choice to choose for delicacy best,
What order so contrived as not to mix
Tastes not well join'd, inelegant, but bring
Taste after taste, upheld with kindliest change.
    JOHN MILTON
    Eve prepares the feast, *Paradise Lost*

*Things not to be forgotten at a Picnic*: A stick of horseradish, a bottle of mint-sauce well corked, a bottle of salad dressing, a bottle of vinegar, made mustard, pepper, salt, good oil, and pounded sugar. If it can be managed, take a little ice. It is scarcely necessary to say that plates, tumblers, wine-glasses, knives, forks, and spoons, must not be forgotten; as also teacups and saucers, 3 or 4 teapots, some lump sugar, and milk, if this last-named article cannot be obtained in the neighbourhood. Take 3 corkscrews.
    ISABELLA BEETON
    *The Book of Household Management*, 1861

The tea had been put into bottles wrapped in flannels (there were no Thermos flasks then); and the climax came when it was found that it had all been sugared beforehand. This was an inexpressible calamity. They all hated sugar in their tea.
    GWEN RAVERAT
    *Period Piece*

A picnic is the Englishman's grand gesture, his final defiance flung in the face of fate.
    GEORGINA BATTISCOMBE
    *English Picnics*, 1949

# Teas

'Ah, that's one thing I *can* do,' said I, laughing brightly. 'I can make very good tea. The great secret is to warm the teapot.'

'Warm the teapot,' interrupted the Herr Rat ... 'What do you warm the teapot for? Ha! ha! that's very good! One does not eat the teapot, I suppose? ... So that is the great secret of your English tea? All you do is to warm the teapot.'

    KATHERINE MANSFIELD
    *In a German Pension*

The tea-things, including a bottle of rather suspicious character and a cold knuckle of ham, were set forth upon a drum, covered with a white napkin; and there, as if at the most convenient round-table in all the world, sat this roving lady, taking her tea and enjoying the prospect.

    CHARLES DICKENS
    Mrs Jarley's bibulous tea, *The Old Curiosity Shop*

... a great cup of American home-made coffee, with the cream a-froth on top, some real butter, firm and

yellow and fresh, some smoking-hot biscuits, a plate
of hot buckwheat cakes, with transparent syrup ...

MARK TWAIN
*A Tramp Abroad*

At Werfel we stopped at 4 p.m. for coffee at an
outwardly unassuming hotel and had superb coffee
and cakes, very well served by a smart, slim,
sparkling waitress. Within I saw the kitchen and a
chef in a chef's white cap making pastry. It was
strange to see this perfection in a village lost in the
mountains.

ARNOLD BENNETT
*Journals*, 2 August 1925

... the ample charms of a genuine Dutch country tea
table, in the sumptuous time of autumn. Such
heaped-up platters of cakes of various and almost
indescribable kinds, known only to experienced
Dutch housewives! There was the doughty
doughnut, the tenderer oly koek, and the crisp and
crumbling cruller; sweet cakes and shortcakes, ginger
cakes and honey cakes, and the whole family of
cakes. And then there were apple pies and peach pies
and pumpkin pies; beside slices of ham and smoked
beef; and moreover delectable dishes of preserved
plums, and peaches, and pears, and quinces; ...
together with bowls of milk and cream, all mingled
higgledy-piggledy, ... with the motherly teapot
sending up its clouds of vapor from the midst.

WASHINGTON IRVING
*The Legend of Sleepy Hollow*

The lower-school boys of the School-house, some
fifteen in number, had tea in the lower-fifth school,
and were presided over by the old verger or
head-porter. Each boy had a quarter of a loaf of bread
and a pat of butter, and as much tea as he pleased;

and there was scarcely one who didn't add to this
some further luxury, such as baked potatoes, a
herring, sprats, or something of the sort; but few, at
this period of the half-year, could live up to a pound
of Porter's sausages, and East was in great
magnificence upon the strength of theirs. He had
produced a toasting-fork from his study, and set Tom
to toast the sausages.

THOMAS HUGHES
*Tom Brown's Schooldays*

High tea at 7.30 and croquet given up. More than 40
people sat down. Plenty of iced claret cup, and
unlimited fruit, very fine, especially the strawberries.

REVD FRANCIS KILVERT
*Diary*, 12 July 1870

# The Art of Dining

Six persons, counting the host, make the right number for a meal: if there be more, it is no meal, but a mêlée.

AUSONIUS
*Ephemeris*

The best number for a dinner party is two – myself and a dam' good head waiter.

attributed to NUBAR GULBENKIAN

Oh, the pleasure of eating alone! – eating my dinner alone!

CHARLES LAMB
in a letter to Mary Wordsworth, 1818

Solitary dinners, I think, ought to be avoided as much as possible, because solitude tends to produce thought, and thought tends to the suspension of the digestive powers.

THOMAS WALKER
*Aristology*, or *The Art of Dining*, 1835

We should look for someone to eat and drink with before looking for something to eat and drink, for dining alone is leading the life of a lion or wolf.

EPICURUS
*Aphorisms*

*Dine*, v: to eat a good dinner in good company, and eat it slow.

AMBROSE BIERCE
*The Devil's Dictionary*

Dined at home; and though I ate only some minced veal, some spinach, and eggs, in moderate quantity, felt myself greatly oppressed, so as to afford a strong instance in confirmation of the opinion, that a solitary dinner, for whatever reason, does not so soon pass away as one ate in company ... Besides the effect that company may have on the mind, much, I apprehend, is to be ascribed to the action given to the lungs and stomach by talking.

WILLIAM WINDHAM
*Diary*, 3 May 1787


At a dinner-party one should eat wisely but not too well, and talk well but not too wisely.

W. SOMERSET MAUGHAM
*A Writer's Notebook*


When I complained of having dined at a splendid table without hearing one sentence of conversation worthy of being remembered, he said, 'Sir, there seldom is any such conversation.' *Boswell*: 'Why then meet at table?' *Johnson*: 'Why, to eat and drink together, and to promote kindness; and, Sir, this is better done when there is no solid conversation; for when there is, people differ in opinion, and get into bad humour, or some of the company who are not capable of such conversation, are left out, and feel themselves uneasy. It was for this reason, Sir Robert Walpole said, he always talked bawdy at his table, because in that all could join.'

JAMES BOSWELL
*Life of Johnson*


Women, who everywhere else provide the charm in society, are out of place at a dinner of gourmands, where the attention, which wishes to be undivided, is entirely for what is on the table rather than for what is

round it. But after wine and coffee, the fair sex
regains its attractions.
GRIMOD DE LA REYNIÈRE
*Calendrier Gastronomique*


A dinner of men is well now and again, but few
well-regulated minds relish a dinner without women.
There are some wretches who, I believe, still meet
together for the sake of what is called 'the spread',
and have horrid delights in turtle, early peas, and
other culinary luxuries – but I pity the condition as I
avoid the banquets of those men. The only substitute
for ladies at dinners, or consolation for want of them,
is – smoking. Cigars, introduced with the coffee, do,
if anything can, make us forget the absence of the
other sex.
W.M. THACKERAY
*Travels in London*


Those who have dined in the very small rooms, called
*cabinets particuliers*, at the restaurants in Paris, must
have remarked the beneficial influence of com-
pactness in promoting hilarity, and banishing
abstraction and restraint.
THOMAS WALKER
*Aristology*, or *The Art of Dining*, 1835


If you are ever at a loss to support a flagging
conversation, introduce the subject of eating.
LEIGH HUNT
*Table Talk*


Conversation is the enemy of good wine and food.
ALFRED HITCHCOCK

113

The other day, when dining alone with a friend of mine I could not help being constantly sensible of the unsocial influence of too large a table. The circular form seems to me to be the most desirable ... For any number not exceeding four, I think a square or oblong table quite as comfortable.

THOMAS WALKER
*Aristology*, or *The Art of Dining*, 1835

Now and then it is a joy to have one's table red with wine and roses.

OSCAR WILDE
*De Profundis*

There were tangerines and apples stained with strawberry pink. Some yellow pears, smooth as silk, some white grapes covered with a silver bloom and a big cluster of purple ones. These last she had bought to tone in with the new dining-room carpet. Yes, that did sound rather far-fetched and absurd, but it was really why she had bought them. She had thought in the shop: 'I must have some purple ones to bring the carpet up to the table.' And it had seemed quite sense at the time.

When she had finished with them and had made two pyramids of these bright round shapes, she stood away from the table to get the effect – and it really was most curious. For the dark table seemed to melt into the dusky light and the glass dish and the blue bowl to float in the air.

KATHERINE MANSFIELD
*Bliss*

The dining-room stood apart from the house, in the midst of orange trees: it was an elegant oblong pavilion of Greek marble, refreshed by fountains that shot in air through scintillating streams, and the table, covered with the beautiful and picturesque dessert, emitted no odour that was not in perfect conformity with the freshness of the scene and fervour of the season. No burnished gold reflected the glaring sunset, no brilliant silver dazzled the eyes; porcelain, beyond the price of all precious metals by its beauty and its fragility, every plate a picture, consorted with the general character of sumptuous simplicity which reigned over the whole, and showed how well the masters of the feats had consulted the genius of the place in all.

LADY MORGAN describing dinner at the
Rothschilds', in a letter in 1828

Dine we must, and we may as well dine elegantly as well as wholesomely.

ISABELLA BEETON
*Book of Household Management*, 1861

It is the quality of the wines which make a good dinner a truly elegant one.

MARQUIS DE CASTELLANE

Food without wine is a corpse; wine without food is a ghost; united and well matched they are as body and soul.

> ANDRÉ SIMON

Lord Monmouth's dinners at Paris were celebrated. It was generally agreed that they had no rivals; yet there were others who had as skilful cooks, others who ... were equally profuse in their expenditure. What, then, was the secret spell of his success? The simplest in the world, though no one seemed aware of it. His Lordship's plates were always hot.

> BENJAMIN DISRAELI
> *Coningsby*

To wait too long for a guest who is late shows a lack of consideration for those who are there.

> BRILLAT-SAVARIN
> *La Physiologie du goût*

One of the company not being come at the appointed hour, I proposed, as usual upon such occasions, to order dinner to be served; adding, 'Ought six people to be kept waiting for one?' 'Why, yes, (answered Johnson, with a delicate humanity) if the one will suffer more by your sitting down, than the six will do by waiting.'

> JAMES BOSWELL
> *Life of Johnson*

On the Continent people have good food; in England people have good table manners.

> GEORGE MIKES
> *How to Be an Alien*

Where the guests at a gathering are well-acquainted, they eat twenty per cent more than they otherwise would.

EDGAR WATSON HOWE
*Country Town Sayings*, 1911

When invited to dine, even with an intimate friend, he was not pleased if something better than a plain dinner was not prepared for him. I have heard him say on such an occasion, 'This was a good dinner enough, to be sure; but it was not a dinner to *ask* a man to.'

JAMES BOSWELL
*Life of Johnson*

Nothing is more pleasant than to receive your friends at your table; nothing more perfect if the food is good; but nothing more painful for them if it is bad. How pathetic that they should at the same time long to see you and dread your cooking.

MARCEL BOULESTIN
*Simple French Cooking for English Homes*, 1923

It is very poor consolation to be told that a man who has given one a bad dinner, or poor wine, is irreproachable in private life. Even the cardinal virtues cannot atone for half-cold entrées.

OSCAR WILDE
*The Picture of Dorian Gray*

Cordiality in a hostess is a very becoming mantle for any other deficiencies there may be.

ELIZABETH GASKELL
*Wives and Daughters*

# Dinner Is Served

Pleasant ... to enter a comfortable dining-room, where the closely drawn red curtains glow with the double light of fire and candle, where glass and silver are glittering on the pure damask, and a soup-tureen gives a hint of the fragrance that will presently rush out to inundate your hungry senses ... Especially if you have confidence in the dinner-giving capacity of your host – if you know that he is not a man who entertains grovelling views of eating and drinking as a mere satisfaction of hunger and thirst, and, dead to all the finer influences of the palate, expects his guest to be brilliant on ill-flavoured gravies and the cheapest Marsala.

> GEORGE ELIOT
> *Scenes of Clerical Life*

What is the use of fish or venison, when the backbone is 6 degrees below the freezing-point? Of all miserable habitations an English house in very hot or very cold weather is the worst.

> REVD SYDNEY SMITH
> in a letter in 1819

At noon I carried my wife by coach to my cousin Thomas Pepys's, where we, with my father, Dr Thomas, cousin Stradwick, Scott, and their wives, dined ... But his dinner a sorry, poor dinner for a man of his estate, there being nothing but ordinary meat in it.... Supped with them and Mr Pierce, the purser, and his wife and mine, where we had a calf's head carboned, but it was raw – we could not eat it.

> SAMUEL PEPYS
> *Diary*, 1 January 1661

The plate was handsome but quite cold; the soup was frozen and the champagne hot.

> HENRY RICHARD FOX, 3rd Baron Holland
> *Diary*, 9 December 1829

If the soup had been as warm as the claret ...
If the claret had been as old as the chicken ...
If the chicken had been as fat as our host ...
It would have been a splendid meal.

> DONALD McCULLOUGH
> 'After Dinner Grace', 1960

Then they went in to dinner. Molly thought everything that was served was delicious, and cooked to the point of perfection; but they did not seem to satisfy Mr Preston, who apologized to his guests several times for the bad cooking of this dish, or the omission of a particular sauce to that.

ELIZABETH GASKELL
*Wives and Daughters*


It was as good a one [dinner] as money (or credit, no matter which) could produce. The dishes, wines, and fruits were of the choicest kind. Everything was elegantly served. The plate was gorgeous. Mr Jonas was in the midst of a calculation of the value of this item alone, when his host disturbed him.

'A glass of wine?'

'Oh!' said Jonas, who had had several glasses already. 'As much of that, as you like! It's too good to refuse.'

CHARLES DICKENS
*Martin Chuzzlewit*


Then the dinner commenced, and had all the attention of the company, till the flying of the first champagne-cork gave the signal, and a hum began to spread. Sparkling wine, that looseneth the tongue, and displayeth the verity, hath also the quality of colouring it. The ladies laughed high; Richard only thought them gay and natural. They flung back in their chairs and laughed to tears; Ripton thought only of the pleasure he had in their society. The champagne-corks continued a regular file-firing.

GEORGE MEREDITH
*The Ordeal of Richard Feverel*

It was a dinner to provoke an appetite, though he had not had one. The rarest dishes, sumptuously cooked and sumptuously served; the choicest fruits; the most exquisite wines; marvels of workmanship in gold and silver, china and glass; innumerable things delicious to the senses of tastes, smell, and sight, were insinuated into its composition. O, what a wonderful man this Merdle, what a great man, what a master man ... in one word, what a rich man!

CHARLES DICKENS
*Little Dorrit*

With less genius than went to the composition of this dinner, men have written epic poems.

LADY MORGAN on a dinner cooked by Carême (at the Rothschilds') in 1828

*12 January 1663*  To my Lady Batten's, and sat with her awhile; but I did it out of design to get some oranges for my feast tomorrow of her, which I did. So home, and found my wife's new gown come home, and she mightily pleased with it. But I appeared very angry that there were no more things got ready against tomorrow's feast, and in that passion set up long, and went discontented to bed.

*13 January 1663*  My poor wife rose by five o'clock in the morning, before day, and went to market and bought fowls and many other things for dinner, with which I was highly pleased, and the chine of beef was down also before six o'clock, and my own jack, of which I was doubtful, do carry it very well. Things being put in order and the cook come, I went to the office where we sat till noon and then broke up, and I home, whither by and by comes Dr Clerke and his lady, his sister, and a she-cousin, and Mr Pierce and his wife, which was all my guests. I had for them, after oysters, at first course, a hash of rabbits, a lamb, and a rare chine of beef. Next, a great dish of roasted fowl, cost me about 30s., and a tart, and then fruit and cheese. My dinner was noble and enough. I had my house mighty clean and neat; my room below with a good fire in it; my dining-room above, and my chamber being made a withdrawing-chamber; and my wife's a good fire, also. I find my new table very proper, and will hold nine or ten people well, but eight with great room. At supper, had a good sack posset and cold meat, and sent my guests away about ten o'clock at night, both them and myself highly pleased with our management of this day ... I believe this day's feast will cost me near £5.

SAMUEL PEPYS
*Diary*

At 11 o'clock this Morning I sent Briton to Weston House to let them know that Mr Taswell was to take a Family Dinner with us to day, Briton returned pretty soon and informed us that Mr and Mrs Custance, Lady Bacon and Son and Master Taswell would also come and partake of the Family Dinner, and they sent us some Fish, a wild Duck and a Sallad. It occasioned rather a Bustle in our House but we did as well as we could – We had not a bit of White bread in House, no Tarts whatever, and this Week gave no Order whatever to my Butcher for Meat, as I killed a Pigg this Week. We soon baked some white bread and some Tartlets and made the best shift we could on the whole … We gave the Company for Dinner some Fish and Oyster Sauce, a nice Piece of Boiled Beef, a fine Neck of Pork rosted and Apple Sauce, some hashed Turkey, Mutton Stakes, Sallad &c. a wild Duck rosted, fryed Rabbits, a plumb Pudding and some Tartlets. Desert, some Olives, Nutts, Almonds, and Raisins and Apples. The whole Company were pleased with their Dinner &c. Considering we had not above 3 Hours notice of their coming we did very well in that short time. All of us were rather hurried on the Occasion.

REVD JAMES WOODFORDE
*Diary*, 29 February 1788


It was a very nice pleasant dinner. No constraint, plenty of ice. Good champagne and the first salmon I have tasted this year, a nice curry, and the Riflemen strawberries quite magnificent … Clifford Priory is certainly one of the nicest most comfortable houses in this part of the country. The evening was exquisite and the party wandered out into the garden promiscuously after dinner under the bright moon.

REVD FRANCIS KILVERT
*Diary*, 7 July 1870

123

Mrs Sedley had prepared a fine curry for her son, just as he liked it, and in the course of dinner a portion of this dish was offered to Rebecca. 'What is it?' said she, turning an appealing look to Mr Joseph.

'Capital,' said he. His mouth was full of it; his face quite red with the delightful exercise of gobbling. 'Mother, it's as good as my own curries in India.'

'Oh, I must try some, if it is an Indian dish,' said Miss Rebecca. 'I am sure everything must be good that comes from there.'

'Give Miss Sharp some curry, my dear,' said Mr Sedley laughing.

Rebecca had never tasted the dish before.

'Do you find it as good as everything else from India?' said Mr Sedley.

'Oh, excellent,' said Rebecca, who was suffering tortures with the cayenne pepper.

'Try a chili with it, Miss Sharp,' said Joseph, really interested.

'A chili!' said Rebecca gasping, 'Oh, yes!' She thought a chili was something cool, as its name imported, and was served with some. 'How fresh and green they look,' she said, and put one into her mouth. It was hotter than the curry; flesh and blood could bear it no longer. She laid down her fork. 'Water, for Heaven's sake, water!' she cried.

W.M. THACKERAY
*Vanity Fair*

# Feasts and Banquets

The dinner was excellent ... the very best I ever ate out of Europe. Everything was hot, quickly served, admirably dressed, and the best of its kind ... The dishes were placed one at a time in the middle of the table, and rapidly changed. Each dipped his own spoon in the soup, dived into the stew, and pulled off pieces of fish or lamb with his fingers. Having no plates, we made plates of our bread. Meanwhile Mustapha Aga, like an attentive host, tore off an especially choice morsel now and then, and handed it to one or other of his guests. To eat gracefully with one's fingers is a fine art; to carve with them skilfully is a science. None of us, I think, will soon forget the

*The Prince of Wales dining with the Sultan in 1891.*

wonderful way in which our host attacked and vanquished the turkey – a solid colossus weighing twenty pounds, and roasted to perfection.

AMELIA EDWARDS
*A Thousand Miles Up the Nile*
dinner at the home of the British Consul in
Luxor, March 1874

As the meat pile wore down (nobody really cared about rice: flesh was the luxury) one of the chief Haveitat eating with us would draw his dagger, ... and would cut criss-cross from the larger bones long diamonds of meat easily torn up between the fingers; for it was necessarily boiled very tender, since all had to be disposed of with the right hand which alone was honourable.

Our host stood by the circle, encouraging the appetite with pious ejaculations. At top speed we twisted, tore, cut and stuffed: never speaking, since conversation would insult a meal's quality.

T.E. LAWRENCE
*The Seven Pillars of Wisdom*
a Bedouin feast

There were men from all nations ... Some lay upon cushions, or squatted round enormous trays of food, and ate thus; others, lying on their stomachs, and leaning on their elbows in the contented posture of lions tearing their prey, reached out for chunks of meat and gorged themselves.

GUSTAVE FLAUBERT
*Salammbô*
a feast in Carthage

126

The extraordinary part of it was, that so large a number should have been served in such a style; tureens, dishes, plates, even soup plates, were everywhere of silver with as many changes as were wanted. There were hot soups and roasts, all besides cold but of excellent and fresh cookery. Peaches, grapes, pine apples, and every other minor fruit in and out of season, were in profusion. Iced champagne at every three or four persons, all the other wines also excellent.

> a contemporary account of a fête given by
> George IV as Prince Regent

There were two tables in the room, one with Monsieur [the King's brother] at the head of it, the other with Madame. Each was set with fourteen covers, which adds up to quite a lot of guzzling, and there was a superabundance of food ... Those pyramids of fruit which mean that one has to write to one another across the table in order to communicate (not a cause for regret: one is relieved that they hide what they do), are too tall to pass through the doorway (our ancestors did not think of this), and a pyramid which was being carried in was knocked by the lintel. The noise of the fruit and porcelain cascading down drowned the sound of the violins, oboes and even the trumpets.

> MADAME DE SÉVIGNÉ
> describing an official banquet in a letter to her
> daughter, 5 August 1671

One day, a naked woman emerged from a great pâté that had been brought in, and dansed on the table. Dinner and supper came to fifteen francs all in.

> EDMOND DE GONCOURT
> *Journal*

Though it was a private wedding, Mrs Berry had prepared a sumptuous breakfast. Chickens offered their breasts: pies hinted savoury secrets: things mystic, in a mash, with Gallic appellatives, jellies, creams, fruits, strewed the table: as a tower in the midst, the cake colossal: the priestly vesture of its nuptial white relieved by hymenaeal splendours.

GEORGE MEREDITH
*The Ordeal of Richard Feverel*

... a silver wedding dinner, for which the table was decorated with creamy white and light pink roses, with silvered leaves. Escoffier composed for the occasion a dinner all white and pink, in which the

Bortch was the deepest note of colour, the *filets de poulets à la Paprika* halved the two hues, and the flesh of an *agneau de lait* formed the highest light in the picture.

LT.-COL. NATHANIEL NEWNHAM-DAVIS
a dinner at the Carlton, *The Gourmet's Guide to London*, 1914

To the sound of funeral marches played by a concealed orchestra, the guests were waited on by naked negresses wearing only mules and stockings ...

Eating off black-bordered plates, they enjoyed turtle soup, Russian rye bread, black olives from Turkey, caviare, mullet botargo, black puddings from Frankfurt, game served in sauces the colour of liquorice or shoe-polish, jellied truffles, chocolate creams, plum-puddings ...

On the invitations which had been sent out, the dinner was called a funeral banquet in memory of the host's virility, recently deceased.

J.K. HUYSMANS
*A Rebours*, an all-black dinner given by a decadent eccentric

Under the brilliant light of the chandeliers, around the table still laden with silver and gold plate, a group of women appeared, dazzling by their apparel and beauty. The guests were by now in the stupor induced by a labouring digestion, but their eyes lit up with instant interest.

HONORÉ DE BALZAC
*La Peau de Chagrin*, the orgy begins

Lasciviousness, lusts, excess of wine, revellings, banquetings.

I PETER, 4:3

# Dinner for Two

Eat, drink, and love; the rest's not worth a fillip.
>     LORD BYRON
>     *Sardanapalus*

... eat nothing but lascivious meats: first and foremost, strong wine, vegetables, beans, roots of all kinds, well seasoned and with plenty of pepper, garden radishes, lettuces, rocket, rapes, leeks, onions, pine-nuts, sweet almonds, electuaries, syrups, juices, snails, shell-fish, fish tastefully cooked, poultry, testicles of animals, eggs, various sauces ...
>     ROBERT BURTON
>     *The Anatomy of Melancholy*, 1621

Three pounds, at least, of flesh which formerly had contributed to the composition of an ox was now honoured with becoming part of the individual Mr Jones.

This particular we thought ourselves obliged to mention, as it may account for our heroe's temporary neglect of his fair companion, who eat but very little, and was indeed employed in considerations of a very different nature, which passed unobserved by Jones, till he had entirely satisfied that appetite which a fast of twenty-four hours had procured him ...
>     HENRY FIELDING
>     *Tom Jones*

*Editor's note: Once his hunger was satisfied, Tom Jones did of course succumb to the charms of Mrs Waters.*

She rang the bell, and a woman … came in to lay the table for two; then she placed on another table beside it all that we would need in order to do without attendance, bringing in one after the other eight different dishes in Sèvres porcelain. It was a delicate and plentiful supper.

When I tasted the first dish I at once recognized the French style of cooking, and MxxMxx did not deny it. We drank only burgundy and champagne. She dressed the salad skilfully, and in everything she did I admired the grace and poise of her manners. It was evident that her education had been in the hands of a lover who was a first-rate connoisseur …

It was near midnight: we had eaten an excellent supper, and we were sitting near a warm fire. Besides, I was in love with a beautiful woman, and feeling the urgency of the moment I became very pressing.

> GIACOMO CASANOVA
> *Memoirs*

You are not treating a girl right unless you ruin her digestion.

> TOM MASSON

I was just putting another oyster shell to Emilia's lips when by pure chance the content slipped out and fell down her decolleté. She was about to fish it out, but I quickly said it was a task for me. It was necessary for me to unlace her bodice in order to retrieve the oyster with my lips from the delicious depths where it had fallen. In the process her naked flesh was of course exposed, but I made it look as though my only interest was in discovering and swallowing that slippery oyster.

GIACOMO CASANOVA
*Memoirs*

After we have tasted a Cup of precious Wine, fed on a few delicate Comfits, and danced a dance or two to the rare Musicke, everyone taketh a Lady by the hand … and she conducteth him to her Chamber.

BOCCACCIO
*The Decameron*

'I'd rather go to bed,' she said …
'If you're tired some food'll perk you up.'
'I don't mean that. I don't feel tired. I mean sex.'
KINGSLEY AMIS
*I Want It Now*

I have always thought that the almost entire disappearance of the small private dining-room from restaurants coincided with the building of innumerable houses of flats, and that the dinners which used to be given in the *cabinets particuliers* are now eaten in flats.

LT.-COL. NATHANIEL NEWNHAM-DAVIS
*The Gourmet's Guide to London*, 1914

# Christmas

The table at which the King sat was richly decorated and groaned beneath the good fare placed upon it; for there was brawn, roast beef, venison pasty, pheasants, swan, capons, lampreys, pyke in latimer sauce, custard, partridge, fruit, plovers and a huge plum pudding which required the efforts of two men to carry.

an anonymous account of Henry VII's feast at Greenwich, Christmas 1486

Suddenly the butler entered the hall with some degree of bustle: he was attended by a servant on each side with a large wax-light, and bore a silver dish, on which was an enormous pig's head decorated with rosemary, with a lemon in its mouth, which was placed with great formality at the head of the table.

WASHINGTON IRVING
*Old Christmas*

The harper at the head of the hall struck up an ancient march, and the dishes were brought in, in grand procession.

The boar's head, garnished with rosemary, with a citron in its mouth, led the van. Then came tureens of plum-porridge; then a series of turkeys, and in the midst of them an enormous sausage, which it required two men to carry. Then came geese and capons, tongues and hams, the ancient glory of the Christmas pie, a gigantic plum pudding, a pyramid of mince pies, and a baron of beef bringing up the rear.

'It is something new under the sun,' said the divine, as he sat down, 'to see a great dinner without fish.'

THOMAS LOVE PEACOCK
*Crotchet Castle*

I dined in the Hall and 14 Sen$^r$ Fellows with me ... We had a very handsome dinner of my ordering, as I order dinner every day being Sub-Warden.

We had for dinner, two fine Codds boiled with fryed Souls round them and oyster sauce, a fine sirloin of Beef roasted, some peas soup and an orange Pudding for the first course, for the second, we had a lease of Wild Ducks rosted, a fore Qu: of Lamb and sallad and mince Pies. We had a grace cup before the second course brought by the Butler to the Stewart of the Hall ... who got out of his place and came to my chair and there drank to me out of it, wishing me a merry Xmas. I then took it of him and drank wishing him the same, and then it went round, three standing up all the time. From the high Table the grace Cup goes to the Batchelors and Scholars. After the second course there was a fine plumb cake brought to the sen$^r$ Table as is usual on this day, which also goes to the Batchelors after ... We dined at 3 o'clock and were an Hour and ½ at it ... I supped etc, in the Chequer, we had Rabbits for supper rosted as is usual on this day ... The Sub-Warden has one to himself; The Bursars each one apiece, the Sen$^r$ Fellows ½ a one each. The Jun$^r$ Fellows a rabbit between three.

REVD JAMES WOODFORDE
high table at New College, Oxford, 25 December 1773


I would not go so far as to urge, with some authorities, complete abstinence from food for twenty-four hours previous to the Christmas dinner, but I would earnestly impress on my readers the need of a frugal diet at breakfast, lunch and afternoon tea on the day itself ... At 8 a.m., only one cup of tea, with two slices of thin bread-and-butter. At 9.30 breakfast: Tea (or coffee), two cups; fried sole; kidneys and bacon; *omelette aux fines herbes*; two lightly-boiled eggs; six pieces of toast; marmalade or strawberry jam; and a melon to wind up with. At 11 a.m., I recommend just one cup of turtle soup, with two captain's biscuits. At 1.45, lunch. This, again, should be a light meal – fish, cutlets, a bird, and a sweet omelette, washed down with a pint of Château Yquem, and topped up with café noir and a single glass of Crème de Menthe. With afternoon tea at 5, nothing should be taken but a few caviare sandwiches. I know that this is asking a great deal of a healthy normal Englishman, but ... if my readers are sufficiently resolute to adopt this Spartan programme during the day, they will find that at 8.30 they will be able to go 'nap' at the most gargantuan Christmas dinner beneath which a board ever groaned.

LT-GEN. GIRTON MAVIS
*Punch*, 18 December 1907
(a take-off of the writings of Lt.-Col Nathaniel Newnham-Davis, of the *Gourmet's Guide to London*)

I walked home again with great pleasure, and there dined by my wife's bed-side with great content, having a mess of brave plum-porridge and a roasted pullet for dinner, and I sent for a mince pie abroad, my wife not being well to make any herself yet.

SAMUEL PEPYS
*Diary*, 25 December 1662

Up, my wife to the making of Christmas pies all day, and I abroad to several places.

SAMUEL PEPYS
*Diary*, 26 December 1662

In half a minute Mrs Crachit entered – flushed, but smiling proudly – with the pudding, like a speckled cannon-ball, so hard and firm, blazing in half of half-a-quartern of ignited brandy, and bedight with Christmas holly stuck into the top.

Oh, a wonderful pudding! Bob Crachit said, and calmly too, that he regarded it as the greatest success achieved by Mrs Crachit since their marriage. Mrs Crachit said that now the weight was off her mind, she would confess that she had had her doubts about the quantity of flour.

CHARLES DICKENS
*A Christmas Carol*

A real old Christmas revel, I can tell you, plays the devil with your liver.

ANON
words from *Punch*, Christmas 1892

It is not groaning boards we need so much as an orderly method of producing good quality everyday food without too much fuss or expense.

ELIZABETH DAVID
*Spices, Salt & Aromatics in the English Kitchen*

# Bread

The bread I eat in London is a deleterious paste, mixed up with chalk, alum, and bone-ashes, insipid to the taste and destructive to the constitution. The good people are not ignorant of this adulteration; but they prefer it to wholesome bread, because it is whiter than the meal of corn. Thus they sacrifice their taste and their health … to a most absurd gratification of a misjudging eye; and the miller or the baker is obliged to poison them and their families, in order to live by his profession.

> TOBIAS SMOLLETT
> *The Expedition of Humphry Clinker*

Bread made only of the branny part of the meale, which the poorest sort of people use, especially in time of dearth and necessity, giveth a very bad and excrementall nourishment to the body: it is well called *panis canicarius*, because it is more fit for dogges than for men.

> TOBIAS VENNER
> *Via Recta ad Vitam Longam*, 1620

The first time I tried organic wheat bread, I thought I was chewing on roofing material.

> ROBIN WILLIAMS
> interviewed in *Playboy*, October 1982

When God gives hard bread He gives sharp teeth.

> GERMAN PROVERB

The English bread, as a rule, is so bad that at our dinner-tables it has been displaced by the potato. The Englishman wants a potato with every dish that

comes before him – he cannot do without it, no matter what other vegetables are provided. The Frenchman, on the other hand, eats bread throughout dinner; and many have been heard to complain that at an English dinner they are quite ashamed of the number of times they have to ask for bread – they can never get enough. The bread or potato thus eaten throughout a meal serves two ends: it supplies the farinaceous element of food, and it acts upon the palate as a sponge to prepare it for a new experience ... Here is a marked point in which the French are ahead of the English in understanding the laws of gustation. They leave the potato to Englishmen; they choose bread for themselves, and they take care to have their bread of the best.

E.S. DALLAS
*Kettner's Book of the Table,* 1877

Instead of those inconvenient and useless centre-pieces ... I would have a basket of beautiful bread, white and brown, in the middle of the table, with a silver fork on each side, so that the guests could help themselves.

THOMAS WALKER
*Aristology,* or *The Art of Dining,* 1835

The last property is, that it be not eaten over new, as while it is hot, nor when it is stale or growne dry. It must not be eaten hot, because it will fluctuate in the stomack, slowly descend, oppilate, and abundantly breed wind in the bowels, by reason of a vaporous humidity that is in it while it is hot, which in cooling evaporateth; and because it fumeth upwards, it causeth drowzinesse, confoundeth the senses, and very greatly hurteth the braine it selfe.

TOBIAS VENNER
*Via Recta ad Vitam Longam*, 1620

Baking bread apple pies, and giblet pie – a bad giblet pie.

DOROTHY WORDSWORTH
*Journals*, 29 November 1801

Who hath not met with home-made bread,
A heavy compound of putty and lead.
THOMAS HOOD
*Miss Kilmansegg*

You are offered a piece of bread and butter that feels like a damp handkerchief and sometimes, when cucumber is added to it, like a wet one.

COMPTON MACKENZIE
*Vestal Fire*

# Beautiful Soup

Beautiful Soup, so rich and green,
Waiting in a hot tureen!
    LEWIS CARROLL
    *Alice's Adventures in Wonderland*

People laughed at me when I said I did not want to dine at a tavern as one could not get soup there.

'Are you ill?' they asked. 'Soup is for invalids.'

The Englishman is a complete carnivore. He eats very little bread, and thinks he is being economical because he saves himself the expense of soup and dessert. One could say an English dinner is like eternity, for it has no beginning and no end. Soup is considered very extravagant ...

    GIACOMO CASANOVA in London in 1763
    *Memoirs*

The diligence being a *leetle* behind time as usual, the soup was on the table when they entered. The passengers quickly ranged themselves round, and, with his mouth watering as the female *garçon* lifted the cover from the tureen, Mr Jorrocks sat in the expectation of seeing the rich contents ladled into the plates. His countenance fell fifty per cent, as the first spoonful passed before his eyes. 'My vig, why it's water!' exclaimed he – 'water I do declare, with worms in it – I can't eat such stuff as that – it's not man's meat – oh! dear, oh! dear, I fear I've made a terrible mistake in coming to France!'

R.S. SURTEES
*Jorrocks' Jaunts and Jollities*

144

*A livery company dining at a vegetarian restaurant where a really 'mock' turtle soup is served.*

We sat down, grace was said, the tureen-covers removed, and instantly a silence in the hall – a breathless silence – and then a great gurgle! – grwlwlwlw it sounded like. The worshipful company were sucking in the turtle!

W.M. THACKERAY at a dinner in the City
*Miscellaneous Papers*

Bread soup was placed upon the table. 'Ah,' said the Herr Rat, leaning upon the table as he peered into the tureen, 'that is what I need. My 'magen' has not been in order for several days. Bread soup, and just the right consistency.'

KATHERINE MANSFIELD
*In a German Pension*

145

# Meat and Game

If you buy meat cheap, you will smell what you have
saved when it boils.

ARAB PROVERB

A tradesman, even of the highest class, has always
'good', 'better', and 'best' among his wares, and to
convince one's self that it is to customers who choose
their meat for themselves that the 'best' commonly
falls, it is only necessary to look some morning into
the shop of any thriving butcher, and compare the
first-rate little joints, without an atom of superfluous
bone or fat about them, which, having been already
picked out, are now set aside and marked as 'sold',
with the others of more ordinary appearance ...

Comparatively few housekeepers, however careful
they may be in other ways, realize the amount of
difference there is in economy between one joint and
another, even when both are of a given weight and
size ...

A tradesman soon learns who are the people who
*must* be well served, and if he wishes to retain their
custom, will take care to serve them accordingly ...

In books on cookery and housekeeping, rules for
marketing of some sort are generally to be found, but
the amount of sniffing, prying, and handling, which
they commonly suggest, make them rather difficult to
follow. In most cases, whowever, no such exhaustive
post-mortem examinations are in the least necessary
to give a perfectly good idea of the quality of either
the fish, flesh, or fowl.

M.M. MALLOCK
*A Younger Sons' Cookery Book*, 1896

Lady (who has been fingering all the joints): *'Can you guarantee this to be Welsh lamb?'*

Butcher: *'Yes, but if you go on handling it much longer, it'll be Irish stew directly.'*

Beefe is a good meate for an Englysshe man, so be it the beest be yonge, & that it be not kowe-flesshe; for olde beefe and kowe-flesshe doth ingender melancolye and leporouse humoures.

ANDREW BOORDE
*A Dyetary of Helth*, 1542


England is merely an island of beef flesh swimming in a warm gulf stream of gravy.

KATHERINE MANSFIELD
*The Modern Soul*


It is only by softening and disguising dead flesh by culinary preparation that it is rendered susceptible of mastication or digestion; and that the sight of its bloody juices and raw horror does not excite intolerable loathing and disgust.

PERCY BYSSHE SHELLEY
*Queen Mab*


Beef ... is an inexhaustible mine in the hands of a skilful cook; it can be called the king of cookery.

Veal lends itself to so many transformations that it is the chameleon of cookery; only pork surpasses it in the variety of dishes it can provide for the table.

GRIMOD DE LA REYNIÈRE
*Calendrier Gastronomique*


... a traditional beef stew which overwhelmed at least three of the five senses, with its rich and velvety flavour, its melting consistency, and its glistening bronze caramelized sauce ringed round the edge with light golden fat.

COLETTE
*Prisons et Paradis*

148

George said it was absurd to have only four potatoes in an Irish stew, so we washed half a dozen or so more, and put them in without peeling. We also put in a cabbage and about half a peck of peas. George stirred it all up, and then he said that there seemed to be a lot of room to spare, so we overhauled both the hampers, and picked out all the odds and ends and the remnants, and added them to the stew. There were half a pork pie and a bit of cold boiled bacon left, and we put them in. Then George found half a tin of potted salmon, and he emptied that into the pot.

He said that was the advantage of Irish stew: you got rid of such a lot of things.

JEROME K. JEROME
*Three Men in a Boat*


Dined with my wife upon a most excellent dish of tripes of my own directing, covered with mustard as I have heretofore seen them done at my Lord Crewe's, of which I made a very great meal, and sent for a glass of wine for myself.

SAMUEL PEPYS
*Diary*, 24 October 1662


Some of their dishes are savoury, and even delicate; But I am not yet Scotchman enough to relish their singed sheep's head and haggis ... The last, being a mess of minced lights, livers, suet, oatmeal, onions, and pepper, enclosed in a sheep's stomach, had a very sudden effect upon mine.

TOBIAS SMOLLETT
*The Expedition of Humphry Clinker*

The crowning point of a Forsyte feast – 'the saddle of mutton'. No Forsyte has given a dinner without providing a saddle of mutton. There is something in its succulent solidity which makes it suitable to people 'of a certain position'. It is nourishing and – tasty; the sort of thing a man remembers eating. It has a past and a future, like a deposit paid into a bank; and it is something that can be argued about.

JOHN GALSWORTHY
*The Man of Property*

There is a certain man in a certain London club who has a grievance against Italy in general ... He tells his tale to all comers as a warning to those who *will* travel in 'foreign parts'. He returned from a long turn of service in India and, landing at Naples, concluded that as he was in Europe he could get British food. He went to a restaurant ... and ordered a 'chump chop'. He had the greatest difficulty, through an interpreter, to explain exactly what it was that he wanted, and then was forced to wait for an hour before it appeared. When the bill was presented it frightened him, but the proprietor, on being summoned, said that as such an extraordinary joint had been asked for, he had been compelled to buy a whole sheep to supply it.

LT.-COL. NATHANIEL NEWNHAM-DAVIS
*The Gourmet's Guide to Europe*, 1903

'Generally I have a lamb dressed quite whole ... My cook, who is a German, first stuffs the lamb in question with small sausages which he procures from Strasburg, forcemeat-balls which he procures from Troyes, and larks which he procures from Pithiviers; by some means or other, with which I am not acquainted, he bones the lamb as he would bone a fowl, leaving the skin on, however, which forms a brown crust all over the animal. When it is cut in

150

beautiful slices, in the same way that one would cut an enormous sausage, a rose-coloured gravy issues forth, which is as agreeable to the eye as it is exquisite to the palate;' and Porthos finished by smacking his lips.

ALEXANDRE DUMAS
Porthos to Louis XIV in *Le Vicomte de Bragelonne*

Three sucking pigs, served up in a dish,
Took from the sow as soon as she had farrowed,
A fortnight fed with dates and muskadine ...
PHILIP MASSINGER

Of all the delicacies in the whole *mundus edibilis*, I will maintain it to be the most delicate ... I speak not of your grown porkers – those hobbydehoys – but a young and tender suckling – under a moon old – guiltless as yet of the sty.

CHARLES LAMB
*The Essays of Elia*

A pig is one of those things I could never think of sending away. Teals, widgeons, snipes, barn-door fowl, ducks, geese – your tame villatic things – Welsh mutton, collars of brawn, sturgeon fresh or pickled, your potted char, Swiss cheeses, French pies, early grapes, muscadines, I impart as freely unto my friends as to myself ... But pigs are pigs, and I myself therein am nearest to myself.

CHARLES LAMB
in a letter to Coleridge

Carving has long been esteemed one of the minor arts of polite life – a test at first sight of the breeding of men, as its dexterous and graceful performance is presumed to mark a person trained in good fashion.

MISTRESS MARGARET DODS
*The Cook and Housewife's Manual*, 1827


We all look on with anxious eyes
When father carves the duck,
And mother almost always sighs
When father carves the duck.
Then all of us prepare to rise
And hold our bibs before our eyes
And be prepared for some surprise
When father carves the duck.

ANON
19th century


We remember to have seen a man of high fashion deposit a turkey in this way in the lap of a lady, but with admirable composure, and without offering the slightest apology, he finished a story which he was telling at the same time, and then, quietly turning to her, merely said, 'Madam, I'll thank you for that turkey.'

quoted by ALEXIS SOYER
*Gastronomic Regenerator*, 1849


I seized the knife and fork and started to carve. It seemed to want a lot of carving. I struggled with it for about five minutes without making the slightest impression. And then Joe ... wanted to know if it wouldn't be better for someone to do the job that understood carving. I took no notice of his foolish remark, but attacked the bird again; and so vigorously this time that the animal left the dish, and took refuge in the fender …

I laid down the knife and fork with dignity and took a side seat; and Joe went for the wretched creature. He worked away in silence for a while, and then he muttered, 'Damn the duck', and took his coat off.

We did break the thing up at length with the aid of a chisel; but it was perfectly impossible to eat it, and we had to make a dinner off the vegetables and an apple tart.

JEROME K. JEROME
*The Idle Thoughts of an Idle Fellow*

In no form of carving, whether of meats, poultry, or game, does the skill of the carver appear to greater advantage than in disjointing wild fowl.

GEORGE H. ELLWANGER
*The Pleasures of the Table*, 1903

Such a bustle ensued you might have thought a goose the rarest of all birds; a feathered phenomenon, to which a black swan was a matter of course – and in truth it was something very like it in that house. Mrs Crachit made the gravy (ready beforehand in a little saucepan) hissing hot; Master Peter mashed the potatoes with incredible vigour; Miss Belinda sweetened up the apple-sauce; Martha dusted the hot plates … At last the dishes were set on, and grace was said. It was succeeded by a breathless pause, as Mrs Crachit, looking slowly all along the carving knife, prepared to plunge it into the breast; but when she did, and when the long expected gush of stuffing issued forth, one murmur of delight arose all around the board.

CHARLES DICKENS
*A Christmas Carol*

The painter … no sooner heard him mention the roasted pullets, than he eagerly solicited the wing of a fowl; … but scarce were they set down before him, when the tears ran down his cheeks, and he called aloud in a manifest disorder, 'Z—ds! this is the essence of a whole bed of garlic!'

TOBIAS SMOLLETT
*Peregrine Pickle*

The turkey has practically no taste except a dry fibrous flavour reminiscent of a mixture of warmed-up plaster of paris and horsehair. The texture is like wet sawdust and the whole vast feathered swindle has the piquancy of a boiled mattress.

WILLIAM CONNOR writing as Cassandra
in the *Daily Mirror*, December 1953

Of the made dishes that belong to British cookery, jugged hare, I think, has the leading place.

LT.-COL. NATHANIEL NEWNHAM-DAVIS
*The Gourmet's Guide to London*, 1914


A Hare being seen near my House by Ben I went out with my Dogs, found her, had a very fine Course and killed her. Dinner to day Jugged Hare, very good.

REVD JAMES WOODFORDE
*Diary*, 16 September 1791


Game draws a large part of its taste from the nature of the soil it lives from.

BRILLAT-SAVARIN
*La Physiologie du goût*


I took my wife to my cousin, Thomas Pepys, and found them just sat down to dinner, which was very good; only the venison pasty was palpable beef, which was not handsome.

SAMUEL PEPYS
*Diary*, 6 January 1660


Dined at the Bullhead upon the best venison pasty that ever I eat of in my life, and with one dish more, it was the best dinner I ever was at.

SAMUEL PEPYS
*Diary*, 1 September 1660


The pigeon-pie was not bad, but it was a delusive pie: the crust being like a disappointing head, phrenologically speaking: full of lumps and bumps, with nothing particular underneath.

CHARLES DICKENS
*David Copperfield*

... This same Claret is the only palate-passion – I have I forgot game I must plead guilty to the breast of a Partridge, the back of a hare, the backbone of a grouse, the wing and side of a Pheasant and a Woodcock *passim*.

JOHN KEATS
in a letter, 18 February 1819

Pigeons are of an hot temperature, and of easie concoction: they breed an inflamed bloud, and extimulate carnall lust: wherefore they are not commendable for those that be cholerick, or enclined unto fevers: they are good for old men, and very wholsome for them that be phlegmatick.

TOBIAS VENNER
*Via Recta ad Vitam Longam*, 1620

Wood-pigeons check and blunt the manly powers: let him not eat this bird who wishes to be amorous.

MARTIAL
*Epigrams*

Ducks, whether tame or wilde, are in no wise commendable; for they chiefly feed upon the very filth, and excrementall vermine of the earth. The flesh of them is neither for smell or taste commendable: it is fulsome and unacceptable to the stomach, and filleth the body with obscure and naughty humors.

TOBIAS VENNER
*Via Recta ad Vitam Longam*, 1620

... grouse whose scented flesh Daudet compared to an old courtesan's flesh marinaded in a bidet.

EDMOND DE GONCOURT
*Journal*, 3 April 1878

'Oh Robert, the grouse has been kept too long! I wonder you can eat it!'
'My dear, we needs must love the highest when we see it.'

# Fish

In deciding upon the kind of fish to be procured, the state of the market should always be considered. The supply of fish is so uncertain, and its price so variable, that the housekeeper will find it to be the wisest plan to pay a visit to the fishmonger and see what lies upon his slab before deciding upon the kind of fish to be bought.

> PHILLIS BROWNE
> *A Year's Cookery*

Compared with the boundless means of supply, and the lightning-like powers of transit, the price of fish is at present inordinately dear. But this is solely the fault of the public. The demand is too inconsiderable to call forth any great and, therefore, economical system.

> CHARLES DICKENS
> writing in *Household Words*

Let the reader think but for one moment of the gastronomic wealth of our country of England, and he will be lost in thankful amazement ...! Look at our fisheries, – the trout and salmon tossing in our brawling streams; the white and full-breasted turbot struggling in the mariner's net; the purple lobster lured by hopes of greed into his basket-prison ... Look at whitebait, great Heavens! – look at whitebait, and a thousand frisking, glittering, silvery things besides ...

And the Briton should further remember, with honest pride and thankfulness, the situation of his capital of London: ... the rapid fleets of all the world *se donnent rendezvous* in the docks of our silvery Thames; the produce of our coasts and provincial cities, east and west, is borne to us on the swift lines of lightning railroads. In a word, ... there is no city on earth's surface so well supplied with fish as London!

W.M. THACKERAY
*The Fitz-Boodle Papers*

Called at Beales in the Fish Markett [in Norwich] and bought 3 Pairs of fine Soals – 2 Crabbs – and a Lobster – Pd him for the above and for some Fish I had before of him 0. 8. 4.

REVD JAMES WOODFORDE
*Diary*, 5 June 1783

The law of Nature which obliges mackerel and many others to visit the shallower water of the shores at a particular season, appears to be one of those wise and beautiful provisions of the Creator by which not only is the species perpetuated with the greatest certainty, but a large portion of the parent animals are thus brought within the reach of man.

WILLIAM YARRELL
*History of British Fishes*, 1836–60

The river Tamar, here, is so full of fresh salmon, and those so exceeding fat, and good, that they are esteemed, in both counties, above the fish of the same kind found in other places; and the quantity is so great, as supplies the country in abundance.

DANIEL DEFOE
*A Tour Through the Whole Island of Great Britain*

Dinner at 8 and a most admirable conger eel. I had no idea conger was so good, or good at all.

REVD FRANCIS KILVERT in Cornwall
*Diary*, 5 August 1870

In the midst of his discourse the bell rung to dinner, where the gentleman I have been speaking of had the pleasure of seeing the huge jack he had caught served up for the first dish in a most sumptuous manner. Upon our sitting down to it he gave us a long account how he had hooked it, played with it, foiled it, and at length drew it out upon the bank, with several other particulars that lasted all the first course.

*Days With Sir Roger de Coverley* (reprinted from *The Spectator*)

I could see dear old Frank standing in the boat, and holding up a glorious salmon, with its silver scales glittering in the sun ... In our eyes, 'was never salmon yet that shone so fair', as we bore it in triumph to our inn ... We carried it to the kitchen, where it cost my friend no little effort to transfer his captive to the cook; and I am quite convinced, that could he have escaped ridicule, he would have preferred to take that fish to bed with him. I am glad he did not; for a firmer, flakier, curdier salmon never gladdened a *table d'hôte*, and there were 'lashings and lavings' for our party of eight, when we met at dinner that evening.

> SAMUEL REYNOLDS HOLE
> *A Little Tour in Ireland*, 1859

Even when he is relaxing Albert thinks about cooking. If he lands a pike he will automatically associate it with quenelles. If he catches a trout he will imagine it on a plate, meunière.

> MICHEL ROUX, of his brother Albert Roux
> in an interview in *The Times*, 28 May 1993

The host, with Italian emphasis, assured me, that he felt great pleasure in being able to serve me with the finest trout. They are taken near Torbole, where the stream flows down from the mountains, and the fish seeks a passage upwards. The Emperor farms this fishery for 10,000 gulden. The fish, which are large, often weighing fifty pounds, and spotted over the whole body to the head, are not trout, properly so called. The flavour, which is between that of trout and salmon, is delicate and excellent.

> WOLFGANG GOETHE at Lake Garda
> *Travels in Italy*, 12 September 1786
> (translated by Revd A.J.W. Morrison, 1892)

... salmon, refreshing to the eye in its arrangement of pale silver and rose, cold as the glaciers of Greenland after its long hours of repose on voluptuous bed of ice. A mayonnaise sauce, creamy and rich, turning the silver to gold, like a fairy godmother of legend, is the cherished accompaniment.

> ELIZABETH ROBINS PENNELL
> *A Guide for the Greedy*, by a Greedy Woman, 1923

Every day between early May and the end of June, every Englishman and woman starts the meal with a slice of excellent cold salmon, accompanied by a cucumber salad ... The French are less privileged.

> E. de CLERMONT-TONNERRE
> *Almanach des bonnes choses de France*, 1920

While Joe was slicing bacon for breakfast, Tom and Huck asked him to hold on a minute; they stepped to a promising nook in the river bank and threw in their lines; almost immediately they had reward. Joe had not had time to get impatient before they were back again with some handsome bass, a couple of sun-perch, and a small cat-fish ... They fried the fish with the bacon and were astonished; for no fish had ever seemed so delicious before. They did not know that the quicker a freshwater fish is on the fire after he is caught the better he is.

MARK TWAIN
*The Adventures of Tom Sawyer*

*May 4*  I went a fishing, but caught not one fish that I durst eat of, till I was weary of my sport; when, just going to leave off, I caught a young dolphin. I had made me a long line of some rope-yarn, but I had no hooks; yet I frequently caught fish enough, as much as I cared to eat; all which I dried in the sun, and eat them dry.

DANIEL DEFOE
*Robinson Crusoe*

# *Oysters*

If you don't love life you can't enjoy an oyster; there is a shock of freshness to it and intimations of the ages of man, some piercing intuition of the sea...
>    ELEANOR CLARK
>    *The Oysters of Locmariaquer*, 1964

The table had been laid, and we sat down to supper. She ate for two and I for four, our excellent appetites being excited by the delicate fare ... We amused ourselves in eating oysters in the voluptuous fashion of lovers, sucking in each one after placing it on the other's tongue. Sensuous reader, try it, and tell me whether it is not nectar of the gods!
>    GIACOMO CASANOVA
>    *Memoirs*

'Here's a delicious fat one, Noah, dear!' said Charlotte; 'try him, do; only this one.'

'What a delicious thing is a oyster!' remarked Mr Claypole, after he had swallowed it. 'That a pity it is, a number of 'em should ever make you feel uncomfortable; isn't it, Charlotte?'
>    CHARLES DICKENS
>    *Oliver Twist*

Lunch was somewhat later than usual because opening the oysters had taken such a long time. Lecoin put away six dozen, but that did not prevent him from doing justice to the braised veal.
>    GEORGES SIMENON
>    *The Rich Man*

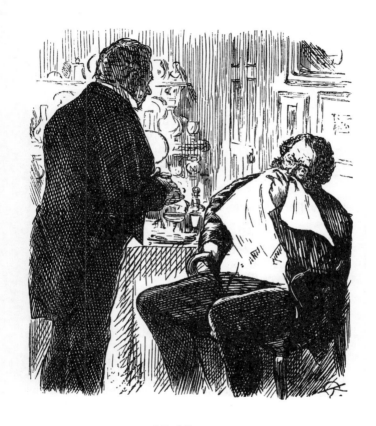

*A Bad Oyster*

'How many did he eat then?' 'Ten dozen every day.'
'Without ill effects?' 'Absolutely none. Nature had
ordered him to eat oysters; they were presumably
essential to him.'

HONORÉ DE BALZAC
*Histoire des Treize*


Englishmen eat it and declare it good; but, as with
salad, they know not how to prepare it. Because it is
excellent in its rawness, they can imagine no further
use for it ... Even raw – again like salad – they are apt
to brutalize it. To drown it in vinegar is the height of
their ambition ... The Greeks knew better.

ELIZABETH ROBINS PENNELL
*A Guide for the Greedy*, by a Greedy Woman, 1923


Kit, walking into an oyster-shop as bold as if he lived
there, ... ordered a fierce gentleman with whiskers,
who acted as waiter ... to bring three dozen of his
largest-sized oysters...

Then they fell to work upon the supper in earnest;
and there was Barbara, that foolish Barbara, declaring
that she couldn't eat more than two, and wanting
more pressing than you would believe before she
would eat four; though her mother and Kit's mother
made up for it pretty well, and ate and laughed and
enjoyed themselves ... But the greatest miracle of the
night was little Jacob, who ate oysters as if he had
been born and bred to the business, sprinkled the
pepper and the vinegar with a discretion beyond his
years, and afterwards built a grotto on the table with
the shells.

CHARLES DICKENS
*The Old Curiosity Shop*

# Unusual Fare

What will not luxury taste?
Earth, sea, and air,
Are daily ransack'd for the
bill of fare.
> JOHN GAY
> *Trivia*

There must be hundreds of unsung heroes and heroines who first tasted strange things growing – and think of the man who first ate a lobster. This staggers the imagination.
> GLADYS TABER
> *Stillmeadow Daybook*

Sumptuous was the feast Nokomis
Made at Hiawatha's wedding…
First they ate the sturgeon, Nahma,
And the pike, the Maskenozha…
Then on pemican they feasted,
Pemican and buffalo marrow,
Haunch of deer and hump of bison,
Yellow cakes of the Mondamin,
And the wild rice of the river.
> H.W. LONGFELLOW
> *Hiawatha's Wedding Feast*

One of the easiest forms of pretense to break down is the pretense of enthusiasm for exotic foods. Just bring on the exotic foods.
> ROBERT BENCHLEY
> *Benchley – or Else!*

The flesh of the moose is very good; though some deem it coarse. Old Hunters, who always like rich, greasy food, rank a moose's nose with a beaver's tail, as the chief of backwood delicacies; personally I never liked either.

> THEODORE ROOSEVELT
> *Big Game Hunting in the Rockies and on the Great Plains*

Giraffe are splendid eating, and in good condition and fat are a luxury that no one can properly appreciate till he has lived for a time on nothing but the dry meat of the smaller antelopes.

> FREDERICK COURTENEY SELOUS
> *A Hunter's Wanderings in Africa*

The fact is, that among his hunters at least, the whale would by all hands be considered a noble dish, were there not so much of him; but when you come to sit down before a meat-pie nearly one hundred feet long, it takes away your appetite.

> HERMAN MELVILLE
> *Moby Dick*

> There was an Old Person of Florence,
> Who held mutton chops in abhorrence;
> He purchased a Bustard, and fried him in Mustard,
> Which choked that Old Person of Florence.
> EDWARD LEAR

The proper way to cook a cockatoo is to put the bird and an axehead into a billy. Boil them until the axehead is soft. The cockatoo is then ready to eat.

> from an old Australian cookbook

'What! This is bear meat, is it? Well, it's first rate!'

I proceeded to demolish the steak on my plate. It was when I was ferrying the last piece of it to my mouth that the landlord said by way of conversation: 'That bear was some brute ... He ate half the huntsman who killed him.'

The piece shot out of my mouth as I felt my stomach turn over.

ALEXANDRE DUMAS
*Impressions de voyage en Suisse*, 1835

In the pith I saw some fat worms or maggots, and suddenly recollected that I had heard of them before as feeding on the sago, and that in the West Indies they are eaten as a delicacy.

I felt inclined to try what they tasted like; so at once kindling a fire, and placing some half dozen, sprinkled with salt, on a little wooden spit, I set them to roast.

Very soon rich fat began to drop from them, and they smelt so temptingly good, that all repugnance to the idea of eating worms vanished; and, putting one like a pat of butter on a baked potato, I boldly swallowed it, and liked it so much, that several others followed in the same way.

J.D. WYSS
*The Swiss Family Robinson*

Dr Buckland used to say that he had eaten his way straight through the whole animal creation, and that the worst thing was a mole – that was utterly horrible ... Dr Buckland afterwards told Lady Lyndhurst that there was one thing even worse than a mole, and that was a blue-bottle fly.

AUGUSTUS HARE
*The Story of My Life*, 4 June 1882

# Crisp Vegetables

A lush profusion of cos and cabbage lettuces, endive and chicory, their leaves and hearts bursting with fresh succulence; bunches of spinach and sorrel, piles of artichokes, mounds of beans and peas ...: there was every shade of green in the palette ... While the bronze varnish of a basket of onions, the bleeding red of a pile of tomatoes, ... the sombre purple of the aubergines added contrasting blotches in the symphony of colour.

> EMILE ZOLA
> Les Halles market, *Le Ventre de Paris*

One of the greatest luxuries in dining is to be able to command plenty of good vegetables well served up. But this is a luxury vainly hoped for at set parties. The vegetables are made to figure in a very secondary way, except, indeed, whilst they are considered as great delicacies, which is generally before they are at their best. Excellent potatoes, smoking hot and accompanied by melted butter of the first quality would alone stamp merit on any dinner.

> THOMAS WALKER
> *The Art of Dining*, 1835

Boiled cabbage *à l'Anglaise* is something compared with which steamed coarse newsprint bought from bankrupt Finnish salvage dealers and heated over smoky oilstoves is an exquisite delicacy.

> WILLIAM CONNOR writing as Cassandra
> in the *Daily Mirror*, June 1950

'Eat up your greens. Finish your greens,' they said to us when we were small. Greens were never asparagus or tiny French beans or sugar peas, but the nastier aspects of the cabbage clan.

JANE GRIGSON
*Vegetable Book*

Cabbage ... causeth troublesome dreams and sends up black vapours to the brain.

ROBERT BURTON
*The Anatomy of Melancholy*, 1621

If Leekes you like, but do their smelle dislike, eat Onyons, and you shall not smell the Leeke. If you of Onyons would the scente expelle, eat Garlicke that shall drowne the Onyon's smell.

*Philosopher's Banquet*, 1633

For it is every cook's opinion,
No savoury dish without an onion.
And, lest your kissing should be spoil'd,

Your onions must be thoroughly boil'd:
Or else you may spare
Your mistress a share,
The secret will never be known;
She cannot discover
The breath of a lover,
But think it as sweet as her own.
JONATHAN SWIFT's translation of one of Martial's
epigrams


Onyons doth provoke a man to veneryous actes, and
to sompnolence.
ANDREW BOORDE
*A Dyetary of Helth*, 1542


Lettyse doth extynct veneryous actes.
ANDREW BOORDE
*A Dyetary of Helth*, 1542


Middle-aged rabbits don't have a paunch, do have
their own teeth and haven't lost their romantic
appeal.
DR. AURELIA PORTER
on why 'rabbit food' may be good for men, *New
York Times*, September 1956


You can put everything, and the more things the
better, into salad, as into a conversation; but
everything depends upon the skill of mixing.
CHARLES DUDLEY WARNER
*My Summer in a Garden*


In a good salad there should be more oil than vinegar
or salt.
attributed to ST FRANCIS OF SALES

172

To make a good salad is to be a brilliant diplomatist –
the problem is entirely the same in both cases. To
know exactly how much oil one must put with one's
vinegar.
> OSCAR WILDE
> *Vera, or The Nihilists*

Their delightful oil and their pleasant vinegar – *almost*
wine, like a lady who has *just* lost her character. Not
the liquid tallow and cut-throat acidity with which
salads are made in England.
> REVD SYDNEY SMITH
> in a letter in 1835

It has been a common saying of physicians in
England, that a cucumber should be well sliced and
dressed with pepper and vinegar, and then thrown
out, as good for nothing.
> SAMUEL JOHNSON
> Boswell's *Journal of a Tour to the Hebrides*

Mr Custance ... brought us a brace of Cucumbers,
very fine ones and the first we have seen this Year. It
was extremely kind of Mr Custance.
> REVD JAMES WOODFORDE
> *Diary*, 8 April 1796

'Tis not *her* coldness, father,
That chills my labouring breast;
It's that confounded cucumber
I've ate and can't digest.
> R.H. BARHAM
> *The Confession*

# Luscious Fruit

Here, as I steal along the sunny wall,
Where autumn basks, with fruit empurpled deep,
My pleasing theme continual prompts my
   thought;
Presents the downy peach, the shining plum,
The ruddy, fragrant nectarine, and dark,
Beneath his ample leaf, the luscious fig.
The vine, too, here her curling tendrils shoots,
Hangs out her clusters growing to the south,
And scarcely wishes for a warmer sky.
   JAMES THOMSON
   *The Seasons*


The weather has become intensely hot again. There
are such quantities of apricots this year and they all
ripen so fast together that there is no knowing what
to do with them. A great number have been given
away.
   REVD FRANCIS KILVERT
   *Diary*, 11 August 1870


I should like now to promenade round you Gardens –
apple tasting – pear-tasting – plum judging – apricot
nibbling – peach scrunching – Nectarine-sucking and
Melon carving – I have also a great feeling for
antiquated cherries full of sugar cracks – and a white
currant tree kept for company.
   JOHN KEATS
   in a letter to Fanny Keats, 28 August 1819


The way in which the fruit is arranged, mixed with
flowers and sprigs in baskets and on stalls, is

particularly elegant. The figs are piled up in baskets, with flowers placed amongst them, which prevent the flies settling upon them. The grapes are carried in baskets on men's heads ... The lemonade stalls, which resemble little altars, are a great ornament to the streets and are decorated with flowers, oranges, and lemons. The abundance of fruit and flowers pleases still more than their beauty. In this climate they are positive blessings, and within the reach of the poorest of the population. The Lazaroni devour the slices of water-melon with greater relish than an epicure sits down to a turtle feast.

LADY MURRAY in Naples
*A Journal of a Tour in Italy*, 1836

They had another special commodity when I was there, which is one of the most delectable dishes for Sommer fruite of all Christendome, namely muske Melons. I wondered at the plenty of them; for there was such store brought into the citie every morning and evening for the space of a month together, that not only St Markes place, but also all the market places of the citie were superabundantly furnished with them ... They are of three sorts, yellow, greene, and reade, but the red is most toothsome of all ... But I advise thee (gentle Reader) ... to abstaine from the immoderate eating of them. For the sweetnesse of them is such as hath allured many men to eate so immoderately of them that they have therewith hastened their untimely death: the fruite being indeed sweete-soure. Sweete in the palate, but soure in the stomacke, if it be not soberly eaten. For it doth often breede the *Dysenteria,* that is, the bloudy fluxe: of which disease the Emperor Fredericke the third died by the intemperate eating of them.

THOMAS CORYAT in Venice
*Coryat's Crudities,* 1611

From Antibes and Sardinia, we have another fruit called a water-melon ... The skin is green, smooth, and thin. The inside is a purple pulp, studded with broad, flat, black seeds, and impregnated with a juice the most cool, delicate, and refreshing, that can well be conceived. One would imagine the pulp itself dissolved in the stomach; for you may eat of it until you are filled up to the tongue, without feeling the least inconvenience. It is so friendly to the constitution, that in ardent inflammatory fevers, it is drank as the best emulsion.

TOBIAS SMOLLETT
*Travels through France and Italy*; Nice, October 1764

Buy apricots, melons and artichokes, strawberries and cream: it's what I like to eat in summer, stretched by the side of a gurgling stream, or in a cool cave.

PIERRE DE RONSARD
*'Odelette'*

176

I came across excellent blackberries – ate of them heartily. It was midday, and when I left the brambles, I found I had a sufficient meal so there was no need to go to an inn. Of a sudden it struck me as an extraordinary thing. Here had I satisfied my hunger without payment.

GEORGE GISSING
*Commonplace Book*, 1887


Always eat grapes downwards – that is, always eat the best grape first; in this way there will be none better left on the bunch, and each grape will seem good down to the last. If you eat the other way, you will not have a good grape in the lot.

SAMUEL BUTLER
*Note-Books*, 1912


Cool damsons are, and good for health, by reason
They make your entrails soluble and slack.

SIR JOHN HARRINGTON
*The Englishman's Doctor*, 1608 (his translation of the Salerno Regimen)


Sweets are strange; a very usual one is a sort of cake with ... the stewed stems of the rhubarb plant whose medicinal properties are well known; yet these prudish people openly advertise the defects of their most private internal economy by their shameless partiality for this amazing fare.

FRANCIS WEY
*Les Anglais chez eux*


*Rhubarb, n.* Vegetable essence of stomach ache.

AMBROSE BIERCE
*The Enlarged Devil's Dictionary*

# Sweets and Puddings

What? Chestnut pudding to follow? I will need to go on a diet to recover from such a Lucullian feast.

MARCEL PROUST
*A l'Ombre des jeunes filles en fleurs*

True gourmands have always finished their dinner before the dessert; whatever is taken after the roast is eaten only out of politeness.

GRIMOD DE LA REYNIÈRE
*Almanach des gourmands*

Once when the Australian singer Nellie Melba was staying at the Savoy in the 1890s, she asked Escoffier to do some *pêches flambées* as the last course of a dinner to celebrate her performance in *Lohengrin* … Escoffier thought that something cold would be more suitable and devised *Les Pêches au Cygne* as a compromise: fresh peaches on a bed of vanilla ice-cream were served with great panache in a splendid swan carved from ice. Melba was delighted, and later Escoffier decided to add raspberry purée to the dessert which then became the familiar *Pêches Melba*. Its popularity has continued to this day, … but unfortunately it is often very poorly imitated, with synthetic ingredients. As Escoffier pointed out, the chef has no redress for plagiarism of his work.

PAOLO CONTARINI
*The Savoy Was My Oyster*

Custard powder … has been one of our minor national tragedies.

JANE GRIGSON
*English Food*

Prunes and custard followed. And if anyone complains that prunes, even when mitigated by custard, are an uncharitable vegetable (fruit they are not), stringy as a miser's heart and exuding a fluid such as might run in misers' veins who have denied themselves wine and warmth for eighty years … he should reflect that there are people whose charity embraces even the prune.

VIRGINIA WOOLF
*A Room of One's Own*

Toujours strawberries and cream.

SAMUEL JOHNSON, complaining to his hostess;
Mrs Thrale's *Anecdotes*

Just as he was taking breath, a *garçon* entered with some custards and an enormous *omelette soufflée*, whose puffy brown sides bagged over the tin dish that contained it. 'There's a tart!' cried Mr Jorrocks. 'Oh my eyes, what a swell! Well I suppose I must have a shy at it …' The first dive of the spoon undeceived him as he heard it sound at the bottom of the dish. 'Oh, lauk, what a go! All puff, by Jove! a regular humbug – a balloon pudding in short! I won't eat such stuff … I like the solids; – will trouble you for some of that cheese, sir, and don't let it taste of the knife.'

R.S. SURTEES
Mr Jorrocks in France, *Jorrock's Jaunts and Jollities*

They bake them in an oven, they boil them with meat, they make them fifty several ways: blessed be he that invented pudding, for it is a manna that hits the palates of all sorts of people; a manna, better than that of the Wilderness, because the people are never weary of it. Ah, what an excellent thing is an English

180

Pudding! 'To come in Pudding time' is as much to say, to come in the most lucky moment in the world.

FRANÇOIS MISSON
*Mémoires et observations faites par un voyageur en Angleterre*, 1698

My Landlady brought me one of the West Country tarts, this was the first I met with, though I had asked for them in many places in Sommerset and Devonshire, its an apple pye with a custard all on the top ... they scald their creame and milk in most parts of those countrys and so its a sort of clouted creame as we call it, with a little sugar, and soe put on the top of the apple pye.

CELIA FIENNES
*The Journeys of Celia Fiennes*
clotted cream in Cornwall in 1698

... Not that apple is longer apple. It, too, is transformed; and the final pie, though born of apple, sugar, butter, nutmeg, cinnamon, lemon, is like none of these, but the compound ideal of them all, refined, purified, and by fire fixed in blissful perfection.

HENRY WARD BEECHER
*Eyes and Ears*

To nuts we do great injustice. We put them on the table as dessert, to be eaten when the stomach is full, and then slander them as indigestible, because the stomach groans under excess of nutriment ... In Syria, walnuts and coarse dry figs make an admirable meal.

FRANCIS WILLIAM NEWMAN
*Essays on Diet*, 1883

# Cheese

Chese that is good, oughte not be too harde nor too softe, but betwyxt both; it shuld not be towgh nor brittell; it ought not to be swete nor sowre, nor tarte, nor too salt, nor too fresshe; it must be of good savour and taledge, nor full of iyes, nor mytes, nor magottes. Yet in Hygh Almen (Germany) the chese the whiche is full of magotes is called there the best chese, and they wyll eate the great magotes as fast as we do eate comfites.

ANDREW BOORDE
*A Dyetary of Health*, 1542

You put your left index finger on your eye and your right index finger on the cheese ... if they sort of feel the same, the cheese is ready.

M. TAITTINGER
the French champagne vintner, on camembert

Diner: 'What sort of cheese do you call this? It's full of holes!'
Waiter: 'Grew-yere, Sir.'
Diner: 'Then just bring one that grew somewhere else!'

For lunch, he said, we could have biscuits, cold meat, bread and butter, and jam – but *no cheese*. Cheese, like oil, makes too much of itself ... It goes through the hamper, and gives a cheesy flavour to everything else there. You can't tell whether you are eating apple pie, or German sausage, or strawberries and cream. It all seems cheese. There is too much odour about cheese.

JEROME K. JEROME
*Three Men in a Boat*

Rosted Cheese is more meet to entice a Mouse, or Rat into a trap, than to be received into the body; for it corrupteth the meats in the stomack, breedeth cholerick humors, and sendeth up from the stomack putrid vapors, and noysome fumes, which greatly offend the head and corrupt the breath. To conclude, the much eating of Cheese is only convenient for rustick people, and such as have very strong stomacks, and that also use great exercise.

TOBIAS VENNER
*Via Recta ad Vitam Longam,* 1620

*Rarebit, n.* A Welsh rabbit, in the speech of the humorless, who point out that it is not a rabbit. To whom it may be solemnly explained that the comestible known as toad-in-the-hole is really not a toad, and that riz-de-veau à la financière is not the smile of a calf prepared after the recipe of a she banker.

AMBROSE BIERCE
*The Enlarged Devil's Dictionary*

# Coffee

There is no part of the world in which better coffee is sold than in London, more especially the Mocha coffee of Twining (which may be purchased, unground, and unroasted at 2s.2d. the pound; whole and roasted, or ground and roasted, at 3s. the pound); yet there is no spot in this wicked world, we verily believe, where coffee is generally so badly made as in this great wilderness of a metropolis ... The best coffee in the world, taken altogether, is certainly made in Paris.

JOSEPH BREGION and ANNE MILLER
*The Practical Cook*, 1845

With great care I roasted a pound of good mocha coffee, and divided it into two equal halves; one I ground in a coffee mill, and the other I crushed in a mortar, with wooden pestles, in the Turkish manner. I then made coffee with each powder, using the same quantity, the same amount of boiling water, and proceeding exactly the same way.

I tasted the coffee, and gave it to some connoisseurs to taste. The unanimous opinion was that the coffee made from the crushed beans was without question superior.

BRILLAT-SAVARIN
*La Physiologie du goût*

Lukewarm coffee is an abomination which should be administered only to spiteful cats and human miscreants.

GEORGE AUGUSTUS SALA
*The Thorough Good Cook*, 1895

Moderately drunk it removes vapours from the brain, occasioned by fumes of wine, or other strong liquors, eases pains in the head, prevents sour belchings, and provokes appetite ... In a word, coffee is the drunkard's settle-brain.

THOMAS TRYON
*The Good Hous-wife Made a Doctor*, 1692

The liqueur, whatever its nature, should be taken, as in all foreign countries, as a *chasse café*, immediately after the small cup of strong coffee, and it should be sipped slowly, and allowed to linger on the palate.

JOSEPH BREGION and ANNE MILLER
*The Practical Cook*, 1845

Cognac – the gift of the gods, the immortal liquid.

ELIZABETH ROBINS PENNELL
*A Guide for the Greedy*, by a Greedy Woman, 1923

Miraculously light *petits fours*, the daintiest delicacies, and mouthwatering mouthfuls … The dessert wines, those potent philtres, yielded their fragrance and their fire, and their seductive fumes induced a sort of intellectual mirage which weighed down hands and feet with powerful bonds. The pyramids of fruit were pillaged, and as voices became louder words became indistinct and glasses were shattered.

> HONORÉ DE BALZAC
> *La Peau de Chagrin*

Men are … conservatives after dinner.

> RALPH WALDO EMERSON
> *Essays*

# *Envoi*

Abstain from beans.
PYTHAGORAS

# *Index*

Chaucer, Geoffrey, 20
Chavasse, Pye Henry, 92
Clark, Eleanor, 164
Clermont-Tonnerre, E. de, 162
Clough, Arthur Hugh, 91
Colette, 148
Confucius, 16
Connor, William, 154, 170
Contarini, Paolo, 178
Coryat, Thomas, 65, 175
Courtine, Robert, 60
Cromwell, Oliver, 90
Cullen, William, 38
Curnonsky, 70

Dallas, E.S., 17, 53, 73, 84, 141
Daudet, Mme Léon, 60
David, Elizabeth, 139
Davies, Robertson, 32
Defoe, Daniel, 43, 160, 163
Dickens, Charles, 25, 44, 45, 55,
    56-7, 90, 93, 107, 120, 124,
    138-9, 154, 155, 158, 164, 166
Disraeli, Benjamin, 49, 97, 116
Dods, Mistress Margaret, 152
Douglas, Norman, 63
Dumas, Alexandre, 28, 150–51,
    169
Dunne, Finley Peter, 40

Edwards, Amelia, 128
Eliot, Charles W., 12, 15, 16, 42
Eliot, George, 119
Ellwanger, George, 68, 73, 85,
    153
Emerson, Ralph Waldo, 187
Epicurus, 111
Erskine, John, 88
Euripides, 23

Farington, Joseph, 35
Faujas de St Fond, Barthélémy,
    48

Ferrier, Susan, 98
Fielding, Henry, 130
Fiennes, Celia, 181
Fisher, M.K., 60
Flaubert, Gustave, 129
Fletcher, Robert, 34
Ford, Ford Madox, 14, 60–1, 65,
    79
Forster, E.M., 35
Fox, Henry Richard, 116
Franklin, Benjamin, 30, 35
Fuller, Thomas, 21, 29

Galsworthy, John, 150
Galton, Francis, 47
Gandhi, Mahatma, 38
Gaskell, Elizabeth, 117, 120
Gay, John, 167
Gibbs, Philip, 41
'Girton-Mavis, Lt.-Gen.', 136
Goethe, Wolfgang, 62–3, 64, 162
Goldsmith, Oliver, 19
Goncourt, Edmond de, 80, 127,
    156
Green, Matthew, 31
Greene, Gail, 20
Grigson, 171, 178
Gulbenkian, Nubar, 110

Hardy, Thomas, 105
Hare, Augustus, 169
Harris, Frank, 68
Hawkins, Nathaniel, 54
Haydn, Joseph, 67
Hayward, Abraham, 43, 66
Hazlitt, W. Carew, 54
Heine, Heinrich, 53
Henry, O., 74
Hitchcock, Alfred, 113
Hole, Samuel Reynolds, 58, 161
Holmes, Oliver Wendell, 92
Homer, 44

191